Castles of the Welsh Princes

CASTLES
OF THE WELSH
PRINCES

PAUL R. DAVIS

y Lolfa

Dedicated to the memory of my parents

Derrick John Davis (1927–1987) and Margaret Valerie Davis (1934–2006)

Neur sylleis olygion ar dirion dir
O Orsedd Orwynnyon
Hir hwyl haul: hwy fy nghofion

My eyes have gazed long at a gentle land
From Gorwynion's grave mound.
Long the sun's course: longer my memories

Canu Llywarch Hen, 9th century

First impression: 2007
Third impression: 2015
© Paul Davis and Y Lolfa Cyf., 2007

ISBN: 978086243 970 5
ISBN-10: 0 86243 970 1

Printed on acid-free and partly recycled paper
and published and bound in Wales by
Y Lolfa Cyf., Talybont, Ceredigion SY24 5HE
e-mail ylolfa@ylolfa.com
website www.ylolfa.com
tel 01970 832 304
fax 832 782

Contents

Introduction

'And the King has heard and in part seen that Llywelyn's ancestors and himself had the power within their boundaries to build and construct castles and fortresses and set up markets without prohibition by anyone'.

From a letter by Llywelyn, Prince of Wales to Edward I, King of England, 11 July 1273.

Of all the great buildings constructed by the past inhabitants of the British Isles, few have gripped the imagination and retain a perennial attraction more than the medieval castle. Most castles are now little more than harsh skeletons of faded splendour, neglected ivy-covered ruins, or carefully preserved fragments surrounded by manicured lawns. Though they differ greatly in scale and plan, they all functioned as strongholds and campaign bases of the military elite.

Castles are a product of the medieval feudal society and were introduced into Britain by the Norman invaders after 1066. They are quite distinct from the military fortifications and defended enclosures that had served communities in previous centuries and which, misleadingly, often share the name 'castle' (or *castell* in Welsh). In Wales and the Marches over 500 castle sites have been identified, a testament not only to the remorseless ambitions of the Normans, but also to the tenacious resistance of the Welsh.

The native rulers of medieval Wales were not averse to adopting ideas from the invaders, and nowhere is this better exemplified than in the castles built by the Welsh themselves, styled on the fortifications that gave the Normans their success in holding down a conquered territory. While the great Anglo-Norman castles of Wales – Caernarfon, Caerphilly, Harlech, Kidwelly and Pembroke, to name but a few – continue to attract visitors, they have to

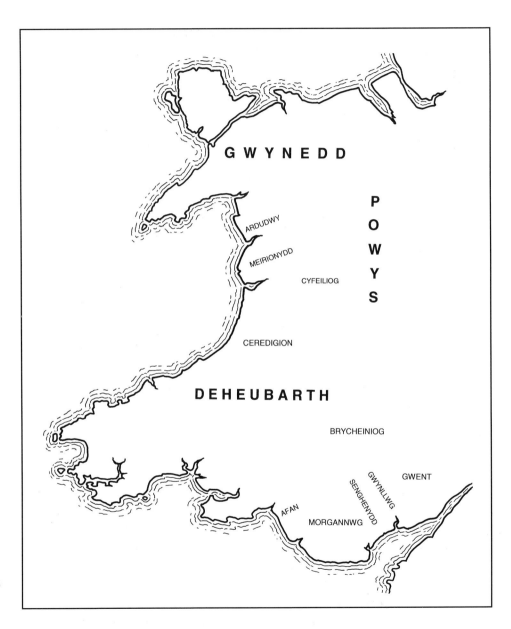

Map of the main Welsh territories mentioned in the text

a considerable degree overshadowed the strongholds built by the Welsh themselves which, although not always as large or impressive, still deserve to be understood and appreciated.

This book looks at all the known and presumed fortifications raised by the native princes and rulers during the period of Welsh independence (roughly 1066 to 1283) and uses plans, photographs and reconstruction drawings to reveal the diversity of style and the individual approach of the castle builders.

Historical Introduction

Wales in the Early Middle Ages was not what we might consider a unified country, but was a land fragmented into separate territories controlled by petty kings and princes. Until the end of the thirteenth century the ruling dynasties of three major kingdoms – Gwynedd, Powys and Deheubarth – dominated the politics and society of Wales. Lesser dynasties controlled the territories between the Wye and Severn rivers in Mid Wales, Brycheiniog, Gwent, Meirionydd and Morgannwg. These regions were further divided into smaller administrative units, called *commotes*, governed from an administrative manor (*maerdref*) and court (*llys*) of the local ruler.

These numerous chieftains were incessantly at war with each other and their own kith and kin, and rarely would they unite for the common good unless it was advantageous to do so. To rule by the sword was the lot of the medieval rulers of Wales. Any unity imposed by ruthless and charismatic leaders – such as Rhodri Mawr (d.878) Hywel Dda (*c*.920-50) or Gruffudd ap Llywelyn (1039-63) – was too fragile to survive for long. A major reason behind the interminable conflicts was the old Welsh law of partible inheritance, whereby the lands and titles of the deceased were divided equally between all male heirs (even illegitimate ones) instead of passing to the eldest son. In the face of any organised foe, this law could only lead to division and weakness.

The principal record we have for this period of Welsh history is the *Brut y Tywysogion*, 'The Chronicle of the Princes', a sort of yearly journal

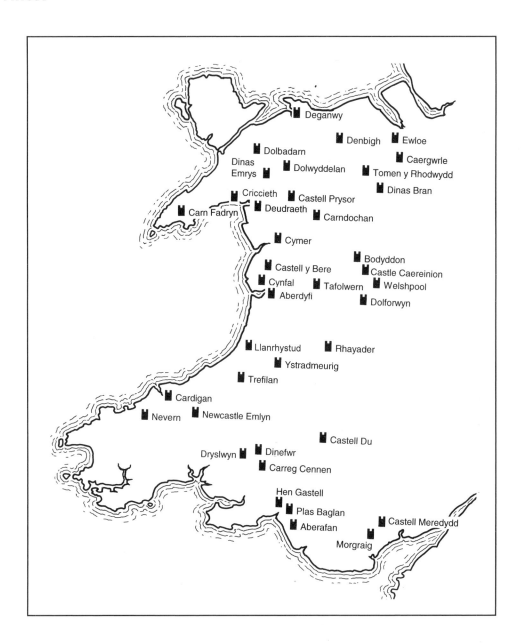

Map of the main Welsh castles

compiled by monkish scribes and detailing notable events from the Dark Ages to the fourteenth century. This sorry catalogue of wars, murders, territorial conquests and internecine feuding can make depressing reading. In an entry for that most famous date in British history, 1066, the chronicles gleefully record the death of King Harold in battle against the forces of Duke William of Normandy. Harold, the last Anglo-Saxon king of England, had been a sore trial to the Welsh in his time; but the 'most noble host' (as the Normans were so mistakenly praised) was about to turn its attention against the divided kingdoms of Wales.

The rise of the castle

The key to Norman success in maintaining a foothold in a hostile territory was the castle. Castles had proved effective in Western Europe since at least the tenth century, and while there is evidence to suggest that Harold's predecessor, Edward the Confessor (1042-66), had allowed some Normans into the country prior to 1066, for all intents and purposes the origin of the castle in Britain begins with the decisive Battle of Hastings. Castles could be set up in a short time to consolidate newly conquered lands, to guard strategic areas, and to act as bases for future expansion. They were primarily the fortified residences of the ruling hierarchy, from where the surrounding territory could be controlled and administered.

With a few rare exceptions the first Norman castles relied on earthworks and timber superstructures for defence, for the lofty stone walls and mighty towers familiar to modern-day visitors were only built at certain major sites in later years. These early castles may appear very modest compared to what was to come and they could only have accommodated a small number of soldiers; nevertheless they were a potent symbol of a conqueror's presence, and reflected the power and prestige of their owners. By building a castle an invader was saying 'I'm here to stay'; therefore it was imperative for the dispossessed to fight back, retake and destroy the castle in order to reclaim the territory. And so it was in due course that the Welsh adopted the concept of the castle in order to meet the new threat.

The castle was not the only Norman innovation introduced into Wales.

Towns and defended settlements were equally important in bringing economic stability to an invaded territory. Many of the present-day towns owe their origins to the Norman invasion, but there are fewer examples of the native rulers adopting this policy of establishing planned urban foundations. The rural economy of the country had led to the growth of scattered farming communities with small settlements clustered around the *llys* of a regional ruler. The itinerant hierarchy would travel around the countryside, consuming locally produced goods at each manor. Although castles provided a secure, fortified residence, it would seem that most of the time the Welsh lords dwelt in undefended halls, and were served by local people obliged to perform feudal duties for their overlord.

The Norman invasion

After consolidating his position in England, the newly crowned William the Conqueror (1066-87) rewarded his loyal followers with the territories of dispossessed –or dead– Anglo-Saxon lords. The Norman freebooters were allowed to occupy and hold territories along the border of Wales, leading to the creation of a buffer zone known as 'The March'. The Norman Marcher lords were granted virtual autonomy in their own lands and pushed westwards into native territory, establishing a series of military bases from which to undertake further expansion. Invaded territories would be further divided out amongst the followers of the chief lord in return for military service at certain times of the year.

Despite the presence of this organised fighting elite and the military trick of the castle, the subjugation of Wales was a bloody, long drawn-out affair lasting just over two hundred years. The story of the Welsh castle must therefore begin with that fateful date 1066, even though more than forty years were to pass before any contemporary document mentions the first building of a castle by a Welshman.

The last ruler of a more or less united Wales was King Gruffudd ap Cynan, whose death in 1063 led to a prolonged outbreak of dynastic feuding. As if oblivious to the growing threat from England, various leaders vied for power in a bloody scramble, culminating in the Battle of Mynydd Carn in

1081, in which most of the warmongers were slaughtered. Out of the chaos emerged two principal figures: Gruffudd ap Cynan of the northern realm of Gwynedd, and Rhys ap Tewdwr of southern Deheubarth.

The fortunes of Gruffudd were the more variable; having barely survived Mynydd Carn, he was imprisoned by the Normans for at least twelve years and later forced into exile in Ireland on two occasions. Yet Gruffudd finally triumphed as the successful ruler of his realm, and became the only Welsh prince to be honoured with a near-contemporary biography. Rhys was initially more successful and staved off conquest by paying tribute for his throne to King William. Like many before and after him, Rhys took advantage of his position to expand his territorial dominions; but after a few years of pre-eminence his power base was slowly eroded away and in 1093 he was killed trying to halt the Norman advance into Brycheiniog.

With Rhys out of the way the Normans pounced on the seemingly defenceless Welsh lands. Robert fitz Hamon swept into the fertile vale of Morgannwg, and confined the Welsh to the bleaker hill country. Roger of Montgomery marched across mid Wales and established frontier bases at Cardigan and Pembroke, while other Norman lords pushed on along the valleys of the Teifi, Tywi and Usk rivers. The Norman presence was already well established in Gwynedd due to the efforts of Earl Hugh of Chester.

However, this rapid onslaught provoked a furious response and in 1094 a series of retaliatory attacks, spearheaded by Cadwgan ap Bleddyn of Powys, drove the invaders out of Gwynedd and Deheubarth. But the Norman grip was too tenacious to be shaken off and despite a further series of uprisings, parts of the country (notably Pembrokeshire, Gower and South Glamorgan) remained firmly under foreign control.

North and South –
Owain Gwynedd and Lord Rhys

In the early years of the twelfth century an uneasy status quo began to develop, as King Henry I (1100-35) relied less on the ruthless drive of the Marcher lords, and began installing Welshmen to rule parts of the country as client vassals under the king's terms. Henry exploited any divisions in the Welsh princely Houses, rewarding and punishing by giving and taking territories, and using shows of military might to terrify any overbearing lord into submission. Under the iron rule of this formidable monarch Powys for a time outshone the other Welsh kingdoms, although its expansion was marred by a series of bloody family conflicts. Being influenced by their more powerful neighbours, the lords of Powys were the first recorded Welshmen to adopt the characteristically Norman technique of castle building. In an entry for the year 1111 the *Brut y Tywysogion* records the murder of Cadwgan ap Bleddyn at Welshpool, where he had 'thought to stay and to make a castle'. Welshpool was to become the principal seat of Powys, and a worn-down earthwork on the eastern edge of town is perhaps that early castle completed by Cadwgan's heirs.

During these years Gruffudd ap Cynan slowly and unobtrusively consolidated his position as ruler of Gwynedd, ever aware of the growing threat on his borders. The Normans appeared secure and firmly entrenched in their strongholds, but King Henry's death marked a sudden turning point in Welsh fortunes. What had at first appeared a gradual, almost inevitable, attempt to dominate Wales was suddenly reversed by a series of violent uprisings.

The opportunities offered by the low ebb of royal power during the troubled reign of Henry's successor, King Stephen (1135-54), prompted the Welsh not only to regain territories lost to the Normans, but also snatch land belonging to other native families. The ambitious sons of Gruffudd ap Cynan – Cadwaladr and Owain Gwynedd – first claimed Meirionydd, and then seized the bigger prize of Ceredigion from the enfeebled dynasty of Deheubarth. The House of Powys under Madog ap Maredudd captured the border stronghold of Oswestry in 1149. Over the next few years the House of Deheubarth under the energetic leadership of a new generation of princes – Cadell, Maredudd and Rhys ap Gruffudd – began to reclaim their ancestral lands lost to Norman and Welsh alike. After 1155 Rhys was left to continue the struggle alone.

The anarchy of Stephen's reign was ended by accession of the Plantagenet King Henry II (1154-89). After settling his affairs in England, Henry turned his attention to Wales and quickly set about restoring authority. In 1157 the king led an expedition and succeeded in wresting homage and obedience from Owain Gwynedd. Another expedition the following year brought a similar response from Rhys ap Gruffudd, but Henry's third invasion ended in abject failure. The chronicles relate how the king 'gathered a host beyond number of the picked warriors of England, Normandy, Flanders, Gascony and Anjou and all the north and Scotland'. Faced with this formidable threat (and believing that Henry intended to 'annihilate all Welshmen'), the princes forgot their squabbles and, in a rare act of mutual support, joined forces to repel the Armada. In the event, Henry's great venture floundered in the rain-swept moors and bogs of the Welsh mountains, defeated by the appalling summer weather instead of armed might.

Henry never repeated the attempt, and his complicity in the murder of Archbishop Becket and subsequent loss of prestige, put him in a more amenable frame of mind to come to terms with the Welsh leaders. Prince Owain died in 1170 and the authority of Gwynedd waned as civil war amongst his heirs led to the territory being split up. His son Dafydd strenuously attempted

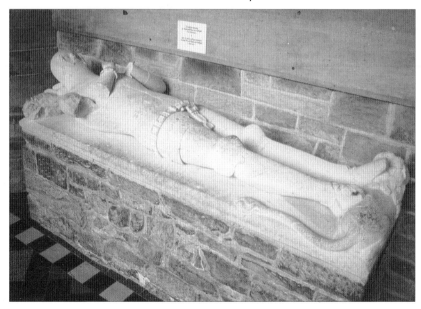

Fourteenth century tomb-effigy of Lord Rhys at St Davids Cathedral

to set himself up as sole ruler but was soon forced to share the inheritance with his brother Rhodri, and the heirs of his half-brother, Cynan.

For the remainder of the twelfth century Rhys ap Gruffudd was undisputed ruler of Deheubarth and the foremost leader of the Welsh princes. With his unservile alliance with the Crown, Rhys ruled virtually undisturbed as 'Lord of Ystrad Tywi' and 'Justice of South Wales'. To his contemporaries and to history, he is known as the Lord Rhys. He was a loyal subject and friend of the king, supporting him in times of need, and fostering an interest in Anglo-Norman culture and society. Rhys

A fourteenth century tomb effigy at St Davids Cathedral, reputed to be that of Rhys Gryg, Prince of Deheubarth (d.1233)

was shrewd enough to realise how much his position depended on retaining the goodwill of the Crown and he made a considerable effort to keep on friendly terms with the king.

Rhys established two power bases in Deheubarth – the ancestral capital of Dinefwr in the Tywi Valley, and the coastal stronghold of Cardigan seized some years before from the Normans. The latter was a strategic site and its acquisition reminded everyone of his status and authority. To reinforce this, Rhys rebuilt the castle in stone and held a great contest there between musicians and poets in Christmas 1176 – the forerunner of the modern-day Eisteddfod.

The fragile peace that had lasted for some twenty years was shattered when Henry died in 1189. Whether he felt secure enough to flex his muscles, or perhaps snubbed by the royal officials acting for the absent Richard I (1189-99), the aged prince once more took up arms against the English and in the next few years captured and destroyed an impressive number of Anglo-Norman strongholds. But a far more insidious threat to the stability of Deheubarth was the internal strife between his numerous heirs. Rhys had a foretaste of events to come when, in 1194, two of his sons attempted to usurp him; but despite a brief imprisonment the Lord Rhys remained ruler of west Wales until his death in 1197.

What had happened to Gwynedd now occurred to Deheubarth, as Rhys's squabbling offspring incarcerated, murdered, or dispossessed each other, fatally wounding the late prince's hard-won unity. By the close of the twelfth century Powys too, was no longer a united territory under one ruler and had been split between the heirs of Madog and Gruffudd ap Maredudd, into Powys Fadog and Powys Wenwynwyn. The southernmost portion was controlled by Gwenwynwyn, a more formidable and independent ruler than the earlier puppet princes of the English kings and who for a time dominated the stage of Welsh affairs.

The Eagles of Gwynedd

While the heirs of the Lord Rhys bickered over their inheritance, the balance of power turned once more to the north, as the gap left by Owain Gwynedd was filled by the ruthlessly ambitious offspring of one of his sons. Iorwerth Drwyndwn ('the flat-nosed') had been sidelined into obscurity by his more ambitious siblings, but before he died Iorwerth sought to protect his infant son Llywelyn by sending him to be raised with relatives in Powys.

When the young Llywelyn came of age he reclaimed his birthright with fire and sword, seizing the lands of his late uncle Rhodri and defeating his other uncle Dafydd in battle. From relative obscurity Llywelyn ap Iorwerth rose to become the most powerful and successful ruler of native Wales, justifiably earning the designation 'The Great'. Through a politically motivated marriage, alliances with certain powerful Marcher lords, and by keeping a tight rein on the more stubborn and uncompromising Welsh lords, Llywelyn used the unsettled reigns of King John (1199-1216) and the young Henry III to extend his authority over much of Wales.

Llywelyn's ambitions were made painfully obvious to some Welsh rulers. In 1208 he seized southern Powys from Gwenwynwyn, and then looked south to the fragmented kingdom of Deheubarth. Maelgwn ap Rhys desperately burned his castles to prevent them being used against him, but this scorched-earth policy was a profitless exercise, for Llywelyn still came, saw and conquered. Eight years later he further demonstrated his overlordship by dividing the contested lands of the late Lord Rhys among his allies in Rhys's family. The dominions subject to Llywelyn the Great comprised the whole of north Wales, Powys and Deheubarth; and while the chronicles lauded him as 'Prince

Above: Llywelyn the Great on his deathbed, attended by his sons Dafydd and Gruffudd (redrawn from the 13th century chronicles of Mathew Paris)
Below: The stone coffin of Llywelyn the Great, now at Llanrwst church

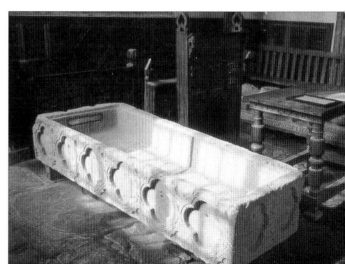

Gziffinuc

Llywelyn's son Gruffudd fell to his death while escaping from the Tower of London in 1244 (redrawn from the chronicles of Mathew Paris)

of Wales', Llywelyn contented himself with the less provocative title of 'Prince of Aberffraw and Lord of Snowdon'.

Llywelyn's strenuous attempt to create a Welsh feudal state united under one ruler, led him to break with the old law of partible inheritance. He succeeded in obtaining formal recognition from the king, the Pope and other Welsh leaders, that his son Dafydd was to be his heir and successor. His illegitimate son Gruffudd was given lands in Meirionydd and Ardudwy as compensation, but he proved to be so untrustworthy that Llywelyn imprisoned him for six years. Even after his release, sibling rivalry continued and 1238 the ailing Prince made a last-ditch attempt to secure a peaceable succession. At the Cistercian abbey of Strata Florida, Llywelyn convened an assembly of all the Welsh princes to swear allegiance to Dafydd. Shortly before he died in April 1240, Llywelyn (or more probably Dafydd acting as regent) finally curbed Gruffudd's wayward ambitions and locked him up in Cricieth castle. He was never to be set free again.

But all Llywelyn's efforts were in vain. The inter-family feuding had weakened Dafydd's position and most Welshmen were too deeply rooted in native custom to accept the new concepts enforced on them by the late prince. Rival lords made bids for power and, as the situation worsened, Henry III (1216-72) intervened and launched an invasion. At this shaky moment Dafydd inconveniently died, leaving the House of Gwynedd leaderless. Gruffudd had already shuffled off his mortal coil in a most spectacular fashion (Henry had taken him away to London as a prisoner, where he died in a botched attempt to escape from the Tower).

By 1246 Gwynedd was back to where it had started before Llywelyn's rise to power. Henry divided the land between Gruffudd's surviving sons Owain and Llywelyn, knowing full well the relative disadvantages of the native laws of inheritance and that soon their younger siblings Dafydd and Rhodri would be demanding a share. No doubt the king was secure in his mind about Wales. Royal forces were once more ensconced on the borders of Gwynedd, and the surviving princes were too puny and

Royal residences

While the majority of the English aristocracy during the Middle Ages lived in strongly fortified castles, the archaeological and documentary evidence from Wales suggests that most native rulers resided in undefended halls within a court, or *llys*, in their respective territories. The *llys* was the administrative centre of the surrounding estate, and would have contained the great hall (*neuadd*), some farm buildings and the humble homes of the bondsmen, who were obliged by Welsh law to provide service to their lord. According to Gerald of Wales the three royal seats of the ancient kings of Wales lay at Aberffraw (Anglesey), Dinefwr and Penwern (a lost site in what is now Shropshire).

There were however, many more sites throughout the country, but to date only one has been fully excavated and preserved for posterity.

In a field at **Llys Rhosyr** near Newborough on Anglesey, archaeologists have discovered several buildings dating from the thirteenth century. The main building was a rather modest hall with a thatched roof and timber-framed walls resting on stone foundations; three smaller buildings stood close by, and one of them (perhaps a private chamber or parlour) was reached from the hall along a covered passageway. Surrounding everything was a well-built stone wall and a gate – not strong enough to keep an army out, but certainly sufficient to deter thieves and create an impressive feature. Had King Edward left the Welsh well alone then Llys Rhosyr might have grown and developed into far grander medieval complex; but with the defeat of the native princes, the site was neglected and eventually buried in sand. Edward even went to far as to signal his victory over the Welsh by dismantling their timber-framed halls and removing the materials for use in his new castles.

Welsh bow- and spearmen as depicted on a thirteenth century manuscript

divided to offer much resistance. But within a few years an astonishing reversal in Welsh fortunes took place.

The ambitions of the young Owain and Llywelyn soon led to dissent and then escalated into open warfare in 1255. Llywelyn emerged victorious as sole ruler of Gwynedd and began the uphill struggle to reclaim the extensive dominions once held by his 'grandfather of famous memory'. Just like his forbears, Llywelyn ap Gruffudd was well able to take advantage of the king's distraction with political troubles in England, to extend his dominions and bring the lesser Welsh princes under his sway. He even forged a close alliance with the king's staunch enemy, Simon de Montfort, the charismatic leader of the anti-royalist faction.

Within twelve years Llywelyn had reached the pinnacle of his success; his territories extended far beyond Gwynedd into Brycheiniog, Deheubarth and Powys, and he may even have tried to seize the fertile Vale of Glamorgan, which had been in secure English control for over a century and a half. Even after De Montfort had been defeated and killed by the royalists, King Henry was still obliged to recognise the authority of Llywelyn. The Treaty of Montgomery signed in September 1267 grudgingly acknowledged his conquests and recognised his title 'Prince of Wales' and lordship over the lesser native rulers. But unlike his grandfather Llywelyn could not deal effectively with the many enemies his ruthless progress had made, amongst the Marcher lords, the other Welsh leaders – and even his own family.

The Downfall of Llywelyn

The beginning of the end for Llywelyn came with the coronation of the formidable Edward I (1272-1307). In 1274 Llywelyn's brother Dafydd and the anglophile lord of southern Powys, Gruffudd ap Gwenwynwyn, launched an abortive *coup* to overthrow and assassinate the Prince. The two fled to

England when the plot was discovered and took refuge with Edward, thus providing Llywelyn with a very good reason not to pay the expected homage to the new king. The deteriorating relationship with the Crown was exacerbated when Edward kidnapped Llywelyn's prospective bride, Eleanor de Montfort, the daughter of his old ally. The prince stubbornly refused to bend the knee, and seems to have wholly underestimated the new king's strength of purpose and character.

Edward's patience finally snapped, and in 1276 he launched a huge military campaign to curb Llywelyn's growing independence and bring him to heel. By the spring of 1277 English forces, aided by Rhys ap Maredudd of Deheubarth (who bore a long-standing grudge against the prince) had recaptured the Welsh territories in the south-west. Other supporters fell away and grovelled before the king. As the armies moved against Gwynedd, the usual ploy of retreating into the near-impregnable mountains and waiting things out while launching guerrilla attacks failed, because Edward sent ships to patrol the Menai Straits and divert the vital Anglesey grain supply.

A modern memorial marks the downfall of Llywelyn at Cilmery

This bitter setback forced Llywelyn to surrender and make what peace he could. By the terms of the Treaty of Aberconwy, Llywelyn was deprived of much of his former territories except for Gwynedd. He had to release his brother Owain (locked up in Dolbadarn castle for over twenty years) and recognise the rights of his treacherous sibling Dafydd. On the plus side, Llywelyn was allowed to retain the hollow title of Prince of Wales and was reunited with his beloved bride. It seems that Llywelyn got off lightly, but King Edward was no fool; to safeguard his position he started to build a number of major castles on the edges of Welsh territory, and rewarded his allies (including the turncoats Dafydd and Gruffudd) with territories confiscated from the prince.

Llywelyn no doubt harboured resentment against his treatment and loss of property, and other Welshmen were frustrated by the increasing pressure from the Marcher lords, circling their prey

Llywelyn's grave at Abbey Cwmhir

The building of mighty castles like Caernarfon sealed the fate of the Welsh rulers

like wolves; but the final act of war came from a surprising source. In March 1282 Dafydd ap Gruffudd led a night attack on Hawarden Castle, capturing the constable and slaughtering the garrison. Why he did this is unclear, but the most likely reason is that the shifty Dafydd envisaged himself as Prince of Wales in Llywelyn's stead. Within days the fires of rebellion spread throughout the land, and Llywelyn had little choice but to side with his brother and keep himself at the head of Welsh resistance.

The furious Edward swiftly retaliated and used the same military tactics employed only a few years before; Anglesey was blockaded and Llywelyn was forced to head south to rally troops. In December a small Welsh force near Builth encountered a group of English soldiers, and in the resultant skirmish Llywelyn was killed – almost by accident it seems, for the responsible knight was at first unaware of who it was he had struck down with his spear. The court poets bewailed their grief and foresaw the end of the world, but others viewed the episode differently. One chronicle of the time gives a tantalising report that Llywelyn's own men had met 'in the belfry of Bangor' to plot his death. Whatever skulduggery was afoot, it is clear that the prince did not have the full trust and support of his allies.

Edward triumphantly displayed Llywelyn's head to the jeering crowds at London, while the body was taken for burial at the remote and peaceful abbey of Cwm-hir in Powis. As the English forces pushed on into the heart of Welsh territory capturing castle after castle, Dafydd continued the war to its bitter conclusion. He too, could not trust his men, and in 1283 was betrayed and handed over to the English. Edward had him taken in chains to Shrewsbury, and there in the market place indulged in an inventively gory form of execution ('godly butchery') to punish the ingrate prince as a warning to all traitors. Choice pieces of Dafydd's disembowelled body were despatched to the four corners of the kingdom. The king was determined to stamp out the princely House of Gwynedd once and for all; those kith and kin still alive were safely locked away in prison, and even Llywelyn's little daughter Gwenllian spent the rest of her long life in a remote Lincolnshire nunnery.

King Edward was now free to consolidate his hold on Wales and continued with his ambitious scheme of building a ring of castles around Gwynedd. Yet despite these monumental precautions, unrest among the conquered Welsh continued for some years to come. The first outbreak occurred in 1287 and was headed by the king's erstwhile ally, Rhys ap Maredudd of Deheubarth. This was quickly stamped out and the fugitive leader brutally executed a few years later. A far more serious and widespread revolt took place in 1294-5 when the north Wales insurgents were led by Madog ap Llywelyn, a distant relative of the late great prince.

By the time the flames of rebellion had been stamped out, to be replaced by decades of simmering resentment, the only Welsh rulers still in possession of their ancestral lands were those who had acquiesced to the inevitable and thrown in their lot with the conquerors, such as anglophile lords of Afan and Powys. For all intents and purposes they were now English lords, subject to the king and bound by the laws of the March. They even went so far as to reject the traditional Welsh patronymic and adopt the Anglo-French surnames of 'De Avene' and 'De la Pole'. The title 'Prince of Wales' was used henceforth by the English kings as a hereditary honour reserved for their eldest sons. Another century was to pass before the Welsh tried again to throw off the yoke of English oppression in one last bloody and ill-fated uprising under the charismatic leadership of Owain Glyndŵr. Of the native strongholds captured by the English during the wars a few were repaired or rebuilt, but most had lost their strategic value and, having been supplanted with more effective fortifications, were dismantled or simply left to decay.

Motte castles at Castell Crugeryr, Radnor (above), and Welshpool (below)

The architecture of Welsh castles

Wooden Castles

The first castles built by the Normans (and later adopted by the Welsh) were smaller and more modest structures than the towering buildings most people envisage. They survive now as denuded overgrown mounds and banks with silted-up ditches, looking innocuous and seemingly incapable of holding off a flock of sheep, let alone an invading force of armed soldiers. But we are only seeing part of what was once here – the last vestiges of what would have been a formidable structure in its day. The mounds would have been higher and steeper, the ditches deep and muddy, and all the earthworks topped with a forest of stout timber palisades and fences to keep the enemy at bay.

The commonest and most familiar of these earth and timber castles is known as a **motte and bailey**. The motte is a mound of earth and stones heaped up in a conical form, and encircled at its base by a deep ditch. Around the flattened summit would have been erected a strong palisade fence, and within it rose a wooden tower serving as the main residence and strongpoint.

This was the last resort of the garrison, safe from everything except fire and starvation during a prolonged siege. Access to the lofty refuge was via a stairway and timber ramp, which probably would have had a drawbridge or removable section to hinder a direct charge. Often (but not invariably) a defended enclosure (the bailey) adjoined the mound, and this too would have been enclosed with a protective rampart and outer ditch. The bailey contained additional domestic accommodation, as well as barracks, kitchens, stables, stores and workshops.

A considerable amount of effort was needed to build a fair sized mound, and in many cases a natural hillock or ridge was shaped into a suitable motte (such as Castell Prysor and Cymer). Some builders took this labour-saving method to the limit, where presumably a speedily constructed foothold was needed to control a strategic area. At Carn Fadryn, Castell Nos and Hen Gastell, the mottes are just rock outcrops of exceptional natural strength, and so the builders needed only to concentrate on digging defensive ditches or setting up a tower on the summit.

The Normans also constructed **ringwork** castles, which consist of a strong bank and outer ditch encircling a small courtyard. Alternately the ringwork may have been sited on a headland or ridge, with the defensive rampart piled up on the side most vulnerable to attack. The weakest part of any castle was the gateway, and excavations have indicated that the entrance was sometimes through (or overlooked by) a substantial wooden tower. Ringworks bear a great similarity to the defended settlements built centuries before by the native Celts during the Iron Age, and can be difficult to correctly identify today. Usually though, medieval ringworks have a much smaller internal area, for they were intended to shelter fewer people than the communal refuges of older times.

Timber naturally decays with the passage of years, and so there are no surviving remains of any early Norman or Welsh castle, apart from the grassed-over earthworks. Documentary evidence and ornate illustrations depicted on the Bayeux Tapestry, suggest that the original timber towers were quite substantial structures, two or three storeys high, and crowned with a fighting platform and battlements. A contemporary description of a twelfth century wooden tower in Flanders reveals

Reconstruction of a motte and bailey castle

Reconstruction of an earth and timber ringwork castle

The Welsh often took advantage of natural outcrops on which to build their castles; this almost impregnable crag is Castell Nos (Rhondda)

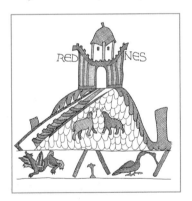

The motte castle of Rennes (Brittany) as depicted on the Bayeux Tapestry. The stylised drawing shows a two storey tower within a palisade on top of the mound, with a flight of steps leading up to the gate

how complex some major timber castles could be. This tower contained a granary and cellar on the ground floor, a series of rooms on the first floor (including a hall, larder and heated inner chamber - presumably warmed by a portable brazier), while an upper level contained additional chambers and a chapel. Clearly this was a major lordly residence, but the relatively small size of native mottes suggests they supported more basic and modest structures. A few examples of relative dimensions will suffice here; Domen Castell at Welshpool rises to a height of about 5m with a summit diameter of 9m; the nearby earthwork at Powis Castle is 4.5m high by 17m across; Tafolwern is approximately 4m high with a maximum summit diameter of 13m, while the diminutive mound at Gelligaer is barely 3m high.

The *Brut y Tywysogion* names some two-dozen wooden castles built, or rebuilt, by the Welsh – the first at Welshpool in 1111 and the last at Trefilan in 1233. There are hundreds of such castles in Wales and the Marches and without documentary evidence it is almost impossible to conclude whether they are of Welsh or Norman origin, although the vast majority are probably Norman. In fact the Welsh never relied upon nor built castles to the extent of their oppressors and preferred to wear down the enemy with 'hit and run' tactics, instead of outright warfare.

Much valuable information (and gossip) about the Age of the Princes will be found in the writings of the Anglo-Welsh scholar and cleric, Gerald of Wales (1146-1223). Gerald described the culture and society of both the rich and poor of twelfth century Wales, and observed with pride the bravery of his kinsmen. They will not hesitate, he writes, to charge a more heavily armed foe, and though they do 'not shine in open combat and in fixed formation, yet they harass the foe by their ambushes and their night attacks'. Gerald also touched on one of the reasons that castles were not always needed in the heart of *pura Wallia*, 'for their country is fortified by nature; they are accustomed to live on very little …and the entire nation, both leaders and common people, are trained in the use of arms'.

The chronicles frequently mention castles captured and refortified by the Welsh but, with a few exceptions, these do not qualify for inclusion in this book; the mottes at Abergwyngregyn, Caernarfon and Dolbenmaen in North Wales for instance, were certainly occupied by the princes but were probably built by Earl Hugh of Chester in the period 1088-94. The same is true of other parts of the country where control of a territory passed back and forth between invader and defender. Even an attempt to identify native sites by suggestive place-names is fraught with difficulties, for it is quite probable that a captured enemy base would be renamed by its conqueror – as Humfrey's castle in Ceredigion was changed to Castell Hywel after it was seized by Hywel ap Owain in 1151. Therefore the timber castles listed in the gazetteer section are principally sites that can be identified as Welsh with a good degree of certainty.

Masonry Castles

Although timber defences were relatively cheap and easy to construct, stone was a more durable material and provided greater protection against fire. It was costly and took more time to build stone defences therefore a prolonged period of peace was necessary before work could commence. Building materials had to be brought to the site, specialist workers, masons, scaffolders and diggers employed, and soldiers had to be on hand while the wooden defences were breached during construction. Work usually progressed only through the summer months, and the unfinished structure would then be covered over for the winter, to prevent frost from penetrating and cracking the wall-tops. It has been estimated that on average, medieval masons could build walls up to three-metres in height each season, although this would naturally depend on the size and enthusiasm of the workforce (King Edward's fortress of Harlech was virtually complete in a mere six years). Welsh masons were not so accomplished as their English counterparts, and relied on their traditional building skills. The varying quality of the stonework at some native castles suggests that 'outside' masons were occasionally employed for finishing the more important buildings.

Usually the first part of a castle to be replaced in stone was the principal tower. This is usually referred to as a **keep**, although originally the tower was

Rectangular keeps at Rochester, Kent (above) and Dolwyddelan (below)

A cutaway reconstruction of the keep at Dolwyddelan. We can see that there was only one main chamber, reached by an external stair, with a privy built into the thick walls

called a *donjon*, (the word only later became identified with the lowest level or prison). In Anglo-Norman fortresses the keep was invariably a massive structure of rectangular plan, containing several floors of habitable apartments and capable of putting up a stout defence even if the rest of the castle had been overrun. Examples of more modest Welsh keeps of rectangular plan can be seen at Castell y Bere, Dinas Emrys, Dolwyddelan and Dolforwyn. During the early-thirteenth century circular keeps gained a certain vogue amongst the more innovative Marcher lords, and the Welsh took to copying them at Dinefwr, Dolbadarn and Dryslwyn. The round keep had certain advantages over the older towers of rectangular plan; it had no awkward corners vulnerable to undermining, and the curved surface was better at deflecting missiles. However, the most distinctive keep favoured by the native lords was a curious hybrid of the two types – square with one rounded end, rather like an elongated letter D. This is known as an **apsidal keep**, and the most intact example can be seen at Ewloe.

Unlike the much larger English keeps, the Welsh examples are quite small and generally contain only two floors, with the principal apartment located on the upper level for reasons of security. The ground floor was usually a dark storeroom, reached through a trapdoor from the room above. Access to the main chamber was by an external stairway, sometimes protected by a fortified porch, or **forebuilding**, which had a drawbridge and stout wooden doors to hinder any attacker.

The principal chamber of the keep was the main residence of the castle's owner and his family. In the more ruinous buildings there is little evidence to show how the main rooms were arranged, or what decorations there were. The floors were usually of timber, strewn with rushes, and heating was provided by a large fireplace or an open hearth (supported by a fireproof pillar from the floor below). The few windows were just narrow openings in the walls, with metal bars to keep out intruders and wooden shutters to control draughts (glass was terribly expensive in the Middle Ages). Furniture would have been sparse, but it is possible that timber screens divided up the interior to form more private sleeping chambers, and the walls would certainly have been plastered and lime-washed, and perhaps enlivened with coloured fabrics or brightly painted decorations.

Sanitary arrangements were basic, to say the least. Latrines or **garderobes** were little rooms at the end of a passageway built into the walls, with a hole in the floor discharging outside. Straw or wool was used as toilet paper. The thick walls also accommodated stair passages leading up to the battlements. It is sometimes possible to detect a row of beam holes below the level of the wall-walk, marking the position of an external timber gallery or **hourd**. This temporary structure was erected in times of war and could be used by the defenders to oversee the base of the walls, and to drop missiles on any attacker below. The holes for vanished hourds can still be seen at Ewloe and Cricieth.

Perhaps the most curious feature of the Welsh keeps is that the roof was completely boxed in by the walls, which carried the battlements at a much higher level. This is in contrast to most English castles where the roof was generally level with the wall-walk. At Dolbadarn for instance, the walls rise at least 3m above the roofline of the topmost floor, allowing enough room for an extra chamber. Why the builders did not utilise this wasted space is unclear, but perhaps a tower with just one residential apartment was considered sufficient for the modest needs of a Welsh lord and his family.

The keep was rarely intended to stand alone, and one or more enclosed courtyards, or **wards**, were usually provided to shelter additional buildings and provide defence for the flank most vulnerable to attack. Many native castles were located on natural rock outcrops that offered great defensive potential, but forced the builders to adapt their plans to fit the restricted site. Therefore the wards tend to be very simple enclosures when compared to the larger and more elaborate English strongholds. The perimeter defences usually consist of straight lengths of curtain wall following the crest of the ridge and linking up with the towers. Where necessary, deep ditches were cut through the bedrock providing suitable building material and adding to

Early 13th century round keeps at Dolbadarn (above) and Tretower, Powys (below)

the obstacles facing any attacker. Massive ditches are a particular feature of native castles and, even in their silted-up state, still form effective barriers at Dinas Brân, Ewloe, and Rhayader, for instance.

Putting a date to these early stone castles is very difficult because contemporary references and building records are virtually non-existent among the Welsh, in contrast to the fastidious expenditure details preserved in English royal accounts. This lack of documentary evidence has fuelled many debates over the origins and evolution of native castles, particularly with regard to Cricieth, Ewloe and Morgraig. The first certain reference to a Welsh masonry castle dates from 1171, when the Lord Rhys rebuilt the Norman castle of Cardigan 'in stone and mortar' according to the *Brut y Tywysogion*. It is believed that Rhys also added masonry defences to the ancestral seat at Dinefwr, but unfortunately none of his work can be identified with any confidence.

The next reference occurs in the writings of Gerald of Wales, who accompanied the Archbishop of Canterbury on a trek around the country in 1188, recruiting men for the crusades. On route he observed two newly built castles at Carn Fadryn and Deudraeth in Gwynedd; both sites are natural rock outcrops strengthened with rough stonework, but are rather basic and primitive structures for such a late date. Similar fortifications at Pen-y-castell and Tomen Castell (the forerunner of Dolwyddelan) may belong to the same troubled period following the death of Owain Gwynedd in the late-twelfth century.

Native masonry castles in South Wales are few and far between, and those that do survive display much rebuilding work after they passed into English control (such as Cardigan and Carreg Cennen). This dearth of large castles in the south must be due principally to the absence of any authoritative motivating ruler (with the necessary cash and labour force) at a time when the Welsh increasingly used masonry defences. We have mentioned that the earliest recorded stone castles date from late in the reign of the Lord Rhys, but earth and timber fortifications were still popular among the Welsh at this time, and very little of Rhys's architectural ambitions survive to be appreciated today. Several generations were to pass before the appearance

Beeston (Cheshire) may have been the inspiration behind Llywelyn's gatehouse at Cricieth

Cricieth: the twin-towered gatehouse

Reconstruction of the twin-towered gatehouse as it might have looked in Llywelyn's day

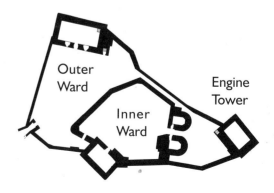

31

of princes rich or powerful enough to order the construction of extensive masonry works in the south.

Castle building in the thirteenth century was dominated by the princes of Gwynedd. In the early years of the century, Llywelyn the Great consolidated his position by building a string of forts in and around his mountainous realm – Castell y Bere, Cricieth, Deganwy, Dolbadarn, Dolwyddelan and probably Carndochan. Of these new castles the largest and most elaborate is Castell y Bere, a collection of various shaped towers and walls scattered over a near-impregnable rock, like a great ship stranded on a jagged reef. The Prince adopted current fortification trends with the round keep at Dolbadarn, which was modelled on the towers built by the English Lords at Bronllys, Caldicot, Skenfrith and Tretower in the southern Marches. In Deheubarth, Rhys Gryg built similar towers at Dinefwr and Dryslwyn, and further east Morgan ap Hywel added one to his castle at Machen.

Llywelyn took a much more ambitious step with his new stronghold of Cricieth, and employed architects to build an elaborate gatehouse where the entrance passage lay between two closely spaced D-shaped towers. The design was no doubt inspired by the twin-towered gatehouses built in the 1220s at the Marcher strongholds of Beeston and Montgomery (Llywelyn had besieged the latter and would have had first-hand knowledge of the effectiveness of such a structure). The twin-towered gatehouse was to become the dominant feature of almost every castle subsequently built, and indeed for years it was thought that Cricieth was the work of Edward I, so typically English is it. The only other gateway of this type to be built by the Welsh was at Dinas Brân. All other native castles had a feeble archway or a simple square gate-tower to serve as an entrance.

The introduction of the twin-towered gatehouse shows the way castle design was going in the thirteenth century. The concept of the keep as a static strongpoint had fallen out of favour with the English and greater emphasis was placed on the overall defensive circuit. Castles were being built with rounded towers boldly projecting beyond the walls, so that archers could defend the foreground with covering fire from strategically positioned arrow slits. Examples of such integrated enclosure castles can be seen at Chepstow,

Kidwelly, Pembroke, Skenfrith and White Castle; but the old fashioned oblong keep still appears in Welsh castles right up to the end.

This difference in fortification design is largely a reflection of the weapons used by the defending garrison: the spear was the principal weapon of the north Welsh at this time, whilst the English favoured the crossbow. Dinas Brân, which was probably built in the 1260s, has a big keep at one end of a simple oblong enclosure, with an apsidal tower midway along one side. On an unencumbered site such as this a more audacious design could have been attempted. A very similar layout was adopted by Llywelyn ap Gruffudd at Dolforwyn, begun in 1273; this too is a relatively simple enclosure with three towers of oblong, round and apsidal plan.

However, not every castle builder was as backward looking as it might seem. In building Caergwrle, Llywelyn's maverick brother Dafydd put into use the ideas he had undoubtedly picked up during his enforced sojourns in England. Caergwrle is typical of many thirteenth century castles where the awkward angles of the enclosure are capped by round towers. Unfortunately, Dafydd did not fully appreciate the defensive principle of such a design. The corner towers should have been positioned in such a way that the archers were provided with a good view along the length of the walls; instead they are arranged in a weak position offering a very exposed flank to any attacker. Llywelyn's ally Einion of Brecon built some sort of enclosure with at least one rounded flanking tower at Castell Du, but unfortunately too little survives to make out the full plan.

Even the last native ruler of Senghenydd in upland Glamorgan included a square keep in the otherwise startling plan of Morgraig. In fact, there is some controversy as to whether this is really an innovative Welsh castle or just an eccentric English one. There are still flaws in the design (particularly the awkwardly sited keep and feeble gateway) but this is no longer a mere collection of assorted towers strung haphazardly together. Here the angles are capped by boldly projecting towers, providing a much more aggressive defence. Clearly the builder of Morgraig knew full well the threat posed by the enemy and how important it was to have an effective stronghold to retain possession of his ancestral lands.

The mystery of Pen-y-bryn

Around 1536 the Royal Antiquarian John Leland travelled through Wales recording all the historic buildings that grabbed his attention. At Abergwyngregyn on the coast between Bangor and Conwy he wrote that Llywelyn the Great had 'a castle or palace on a hill by the church, whereof yet part stands' – but to what was Leland referring? Today at the little village can be seen a small but well-preserved motte, which could be a Welsh foundation, or equally a relic of the initial Norman advance into Gwynedd in the late-eleventh century.

We know that Aber was one of many manors owned by the princes, and that both Joan, wife of Llywelyn the Great, and their son Dafydd, died here. During the war of 1282-83 Archbishop Pecham met to negotiate with Llywelyn at 'Garthcelyn', which apparently lay very near Aber. Medieval documents explain that tenants of the manor provided the itinerant court with consumable goods, and were also obliged to repair Llywelyn's hall, known as *Y Tir Hir* (the long house).

Local tradition identifies Pen-y-Bryn as the site of the manor instead of the motte in the village. This impressive late-sixteenth century house lies on high ground to the east, and has a curious round tower adjoining one end. Experts think this might be a folly tower, a staircase, or even a dovecot, but the present owners are convinced that it is a watchtower connected with the early manor. Traces of ditches have been detected in the vicinity, and recent excavations in the courtyard produced foundations of long demolished buildings and many carved stones. Strangest of all is the large barn, which shows signs of rebuilding, and has a curious series of windows formed from massive slabs of gritstone. Could this building with its great doorways and massive roof beams have originally been the gatehouse to the vanished court? Only future excavations might unravel the mystery of Pen-y-Bryn.

Archaeology and castles

Many old buildings, whether they are castles, abbeys or stately homes, display their evolution clearly in stone; their history can be deciphered by looking at the changes in masonry, the differing details, or varying architectural styles, and so we can understand how they developed over the years. But what of those buildings that have not survived to any significant degree? In such cases only archaeological excavation may fill in the gaps in our knowledge. Several Welsh castles were so poorly preserved and buried in centuries of debris that only the excavator's trowel revealed their plan. Recent large-scale excavations were carried out at Dolforwyn and Dryslwyn by CADW, the government body responsible for the care and preservation of historic sites in Wales. Before the archaeologists got to work only stony earthworks and half-buried fragments could be seen; but years later the foundations have been laid bare and we can appreciate the complex nature of thirteenth century castle design. Finds from previous digs at Castell y Bere and Cricieth reveal the wealth of finely carved stonework that once graced these grim buildings.

Thanks to archaeologists we know that the medieval castles at Deganwy, Dinas Emrys and Hen Gastell, were occupied as far back as Roman times and the Dark Ages. In contrast, recent excavations at Mathrafal (Meifod) have demolished the long-held tradition that this was the ancient capital of Powys established in the seventh century AD. The large rectangular enclosure was thought to be the remains of the Dark Age court; but excavations revealed it to be a medieval manor built long after the adjoining motte had been destroyed by King John in 1212.

Castles of the Princes of Gwynedd

Caergwrle

The Lordship of Hope was among the territories that King Edward I granted to Dafydd ap Gruffudd as a reward for turning against his brother Llywelyn in the war of 1276-7. To safeguard his newly acquired land, Dafydd began to build a castle on a steep hill above the river Alun, on a site fortified during the Iron Age over a thousand years earlier. Llywelyn's scheming brother was

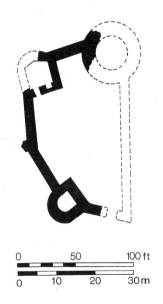

0 50 100 ft
0 10 20 30 m

Caergwrle

This reconstruction of Caergwrle shows the castle as it might have looked if completed. It is not certain if the great round keep was ever finished, and the form of the gateway is conjectural

evidently in favour with the king to be allowed to build a castle so close to the border with England, and the royal stronghold of Chester. Edward gave him money to help with the building works, and perhaps even loaned the services of skilled masons; but it is likely that the castle was still incomplete when Dafydd carried out an astonishing volte-face and attacked nearby Hawarden, sparking off the final war of 1282-83.

The Welsh decided to abandon Caergwrle and withdraw to the mountains, and so the unfinished structure was partly demolished. Within a week of the English forces taking over the site, repairs were begun under the supervision of Master James of St George (the architectural genius responsible for most of Edward's great castles). However, it is clear from expenditure accounts that the bulk of the existing structure was Welsh, and that the English work consisted mostly of timber buildings in the interior, including a chapel and a 'chamber over the gate'. In 1284 Edward granted Caergwrle to Queen Eleanor, but while staying there the royal couple were endangered when an accidental fire swept through the building. Little seems to have been done to repair the damage, and by 1335 the castle was described as ruinous.

Today a path winds up from the village and passes through the woods before emerging onto the open hilltop. Around the edge of the plateau may be glimpsed the worn-down outer rampart of the Iron Age fort, with the more prominent earthworks and ditches sheltering the medieval castle on the highest and most secure part of the hill. Beyond the ditch stand the few surviving fragments of the masonry defences, which still rise almost to battlement level in places.

The plan comprises a narrow angular enclosure backing against a precipitous fall to the valley below, and the confined space and high walls must have made Caergwrle a very claustrophobic and gloomy little fortress. Recent excavations in the courtyard have uncovered the well, an oven, and the footings of stone or timber-framed buildings set against the inner walls. Two small apsidal towers faced the landward approach, and there was a huge round keep tucked into one corner. Only the slightest foundations now remain of this, and it is thought likely that it was never completed (there is an account of the English builders having to demolish whatever was standing here when they took over the castle). There is no sign of a wall along the open flank facing the steep drop and perhaps this too, was never built, or else has fallen away down the slope. The best preserved tower stands at the northern end of the courtyard and had a dark basement store with a habitable upper chamber provided with a large fireplace, and a pair of garderobes reached along a wall passage. From outside the castle it is easy to see the double chutes of the primitive WCs, discharging uncomfortably close to the main gateway! Although no trace now remains of the entrance it must have been squeezed into the space between this tower and the edge of the hill, and a prominent mound outside the walls would have supported the timber bridge crossing the ditch.

Access: The castle is freely accessible and can be reached by a footpath from the war memorial in Caergwrle village, which lies between Mold and Wrexham on the A541 (OS map ref: SJ 307 572).

Carndochan

History and tradition are silent about this remote, ruinous site. It is almost certainly a native castle dating from the thirteenth century, and was probably constructed by Llywelyn the Great, in order to control the mountain pass from Bala to Dolgellau. Only mounds of tumbled stone with some exposed wall-faces can now be seen on this windswept ridge. The plan suggests there was an oval courtyard with a square tower in the centre, and a round tower overlooking the sheer drop to the Lliw valley. The principal accommodation here was provided by a large apsidal keep jutting out towards the more vulnerable southern approach. A rock-cut ditch further protected this flank of the castle. The masonry of the keep is of better quality than the other buildings here and it may have been built at a different period, or else was constructed by skilled masons specifically brought in for the task (rather than local labourers). There is now no sign of an entrance, although it must have been close to the keep and was perhaps through a small projecting tower, now reduced to a shapeless heap of rubble. Virtually nothing is known about Castell Carndochan, but explorations carried out here in the eighteenth and

0		50		100 ft

0	10	20	30 m

A conjectural reconstruction of Castell Carndochan

nineteenth centuries uncovered some bones, blackened soil and charcoal, suggesting that this enigmatic fortress came to a violent and fiery end.

Access: the ruins lie at the end of a rocky ridge overlooking the Lliw valley, about 3km west of Llanuwchllyn, Bala. Follow signs to Dolhendre, cross over the river and take the forestry track that lies beneath the ridge. Access to the castle is a rather strenuous climb up through the forestry and then out across the open moors (OS map ref: SH 847 307).

Carn Fadryn

The rocky hill of Carn Fadryn rises like an extinct volcano from the surrounding countryside of the Lleyn Peninsula. Around the time of the Roman occupation of Wales, the summit was occupied by a large settlement and the tumbled stone ramparts and hut foundations can still be seen today. On the highest peak, a narrow rocky outcrop was utilised as a ready-made motte with a small adjoining courtyard enclosed by a thick drystone wall. There are no traces of internal buildings and any accommodation here must have been basic to say the least. The foundations of several rectangular huts on the more sheltered east side of the summit may also be medieval.

In the course of his travels in 1188, Gerald of Wales passed close by and noted that 'two stone castles have newly been erected; one called Deudraith ...and the other named Carn Madryn, the property of the sons of Owen'. Both castles belonged to the troubled period following the death of Owain Gwynedd, and the likely builder of Carn Fadryn was Rhodri ap Owain (d.1195). If this was the site Gerald referred to, then it was exceptionally primitive for such a late date, and has more similarities to an Iron Age or Dark Age fortification than a twelfth century castle.

Access: Carn Fadryn can be reached by a stiff climb up from Garn village, just off the B4415 road from Pwllheli to Aberdaron (OS map ref: SH 278 353).

Castell y Bere

This is the largest and most elaborate of the native strongholds in North Wales, and it was built as a result of a dispute between Llywelyn the Great and his illegitimate son Gruffudd. Gruffudd had been given control of Meirionydd and Ardudwy, but turned out to be such a difficult ruler that Llywelyn was forced to imprison him and reclaim the territories in 1221. According to the chronicles Llywelyn then 'began to build a castle there for himself'. The site chosen for this new fortress was an elongated rock outcrop in the upper Dysynni valley, from which the lands between the Dyfi and Mawddach estuaries, and the mountain road over Cadair Idris to Dolgellau could be controlled.

This was the last stronghold of Dafydd ap Gruffudd, who struggled vainly to keep the rebellion alive after his brother's death in December 1282. One by one the other Welsh castles fell to the forces of King Edward, before the beleaguered garrison finally gave up the fight and surrendered on 25 April 1283. English forces took over the castle and carried out some repairs, while a small town was established close by in a forlorn effort to boost the economy in this remote, mountainous area. But despite the King's attempts to forcibly quell any resistance, the Welsh rebelled in 1294 under the leadership of the self-proclaimed Prince of Wales, Madog ap Llywelyn. By the time the revolt was stamped out the following year, Castell y Bere had been reduced to a gutted shell and was never re-occupied.

The castle is little more than a hodgepodge of towers and walls tailored to fit the uneven and irregular rock, and its greatest strength lay in the almost unassailable craggy site. Construction work probably continued piecemeal throughout the thirteenth century by Llywelyn and his descendants, for there are clear signs of alterations and additions pointing to a complex building history. It may never be possible to untangle the exact sequence of work, nor identify who was responsible for what; but a suggested development can be offered here. First to be built was the rectangular keep on the highest part of the rock, followed by a curtain wall enclosing the main courtyard and incorporating a gateway, a round flanking tower and a second keep of apsidal

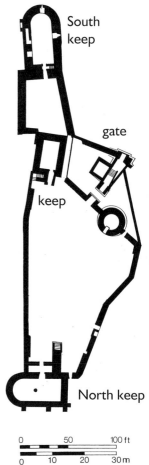

plan, situated at the extreme northern end of the site. None of the walls survive above first-floor level and so the arrangement of the upper rooms is lost to us. The apsidal tower is usually claimed to have been a chapel, but it seems far more likely to have formed the principal residential apartment. The base of a pillar can be seen, which could have supported a first-floor hearth (again suggesting domestic, rather than ecclesiastical usage).

This is likely to have been the first phase of Llywelyn's castle; enhanced entry defences represent the next stage. Anyone trying to force their way in would have had to cross a rock-cut ditch, break through the wooden doors and portcullis of the first gatetower, then charge up a stepped ramp to face

Reconstruction drawing of Castell y Bere

another drawbridge, gate and portcullis, all the time coming under attack from soldiers stationed on the battlements and on the roof of a third tower beside the ramp.

The next stage in the castle's development is represented by its most unique feature – another apsidal keep, set *outside* the existing defences at the forward point of the rock. There was no access to this tower from the rest of the castle (proving it to be an addition), and so a narrow passageway was awkwardly contrived alongside the rectangular keep leading to a timber bridge that crossed a deep ditch. The tower differs in certain details from its northern companion, and could well have

Castell y Bere: broken foundations on a remote rock

been the work of Llywelyn ap Gruffudd. This was the last refuge in the event of a siege, and was capable of holding out even if the rest of the castle had fallen to an enemy. However, it was principally designed for domestic use and would have been the private retreat of the lord of Castell y Bere. The interior is a single large ground floor room, amply provided with windows, a garderobe and warmed by an open hearth – all the comforts a medieval ruler would expect. After the English took over the castle this tower was linked to the rest of the defences by a strong curtain wall.

The unparalleled quality of finds from various excavations at Castell y Bere confirms that aesthetic considerations came a close second to military needs. Floors were laid with decorated tiles, some windows were graced with stained glass, and stone carvings of armed soldiers flanked the doorways.

Access: the castle is in the care of CADW and is freely accessible. It lies 15 km north-east of Tywyn, in the foothills of Cadair Idris, and can be reached along a signposted road from the village of Abergynolwyn off the B4405 to Dolgellau (OS map ref: SH 667 085).

Castell Prysor

No documents survive to outline the history of this remote and odd site, other than a letter written from here by Edward I in 1284. Presumably the king was encamped in the vicinity, for it is hard to imagine this small castle affording much in the way of domestic comfort to a visiting monarch. Castell Prysor is basically a motte and bailey, with the mound being a natural rocky knoll heightened with rubble and faced with drystone. Although it is now very ruined, it is still possible to see the remains of well-laid stonework that formerly encased the outcrop. There must have been a stone keep on the summit originally, perhaps reached by a flight of steps curving up the steep sides of the mound, although whether the tower was round or square is now difficult to say. At the base of the knoll two rubble banks link up with rock outcrops to create an oval bailey so small as to be practically useless – it could only have functioned as a barbican or outwork to the motte stair.

Apart from the presumed tower, accommodation here was provided by several rectangular buildings and enclosures grouped about the base of the mound. They have all been reduced to stony foundations, and it is possible that the vanished upper walls were originally timber-framed. The outlines of two houses can be traced on the west side of the mound, with a third on the east (although this one is better preserved and could be the remains of a later farmstead).

Who built Castell Prysor? It has been suggested that this was the fort Llywelyn the Great started to build in 1221 (rather than Castell y Bere), but this is most improbable; although the Welsh continued to use motte and baileys well into the thirteenth century, the primitive structure of Castell Prysor makes it likely to predate the reign of that great castle builder. If the keep were indeed circular then it would point to an early-thirteenth century date, when such structures

Castell Prysor; the stone foundations in the foreground belong to a later building

began to appear. A more likely scenario is that the castle was built in the politically unsettled years following the death of Owain Gwynedd, when North Wales was divided between his surviving sons. Gruffudd ruled this part of the land, and his brother Maredudd built Deudraeth castle around 1188 according to Gerald of Wales. It may be that Gruffudd, too, felt a castle to be a necessary precaution and so built Prysor, using a combination of the familiar motte and bailey plan with 'new style' masonry defences.

Access: the castle is on private land in Cwm Prysor, 5 km east of Trawsfynydd on the A4212 to Bal, but can be clearly seen across the river from the roadside (OS map ref: SH 758 369).

Cricieth

This 'bright fortress on the cliff top' (so praised in a fourteenth century poem), was built by Llywelyn the Great sometime in the 1230s, on a rocky headland overlooking the sea. The earliest documentary reference to the castle occurs in 1239, when Llywelyn imprisoned his unruly son Gruffudd there; Cricieth was again mentioned as a prison in 1259 when Llywelyn ap Gruffudd locked up Maredudd ap Rhys of Deheubarth for a few months, as punishment for switching loyalties. Following Llywelyn's downfall, Edward I took over the castle and spent a sizeable sum in repairing and improving the defences. Because it could be supplied by sea the castle endured Madog's uprising in 1294-95 and remained in use throughout the fourteenth century, but during Owain Glyndŵr's revolt it was gutted by fire and left in ruins.

The principal feature of Cricieth is the large gatehouse, which survives fairly intact and frowns down on the little coastal village huddled at the foot of the rock. It is a typical structure of the early-thirteenth century and has an entrance passage between two D-shaped towers, protected by a portcullis and wooden gates. There were guardrooms on either side of the entryway with strategically placed arrow loops facing the direction of any likely attack. The two upper floors contained large chambers spanning the width of the building, and the room directly above the passage would have contained

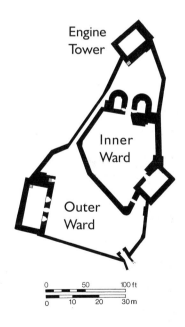

Engine Tower

Inner Ward

Outer Ward

0   50   100 ft
0 10 20   30 m

the mechanism for raising and lowering the portcullis. A broken crucifix was discovered amongst the charred rubble suggesting that there was a small chapel in one of the upper levels. Curiously, there are no windows or arrow-loops in these upper rooms facing outwards, thereby reducing the optimum effectiveness of the gatehouse – presumably the architect hadn't fully worked out the defensive potential of such a structure.

The gatehouse led into the small and compact inner ward, where there were stone or timber-framed buildings lining the courtyard, and a large oblong tower jutting out from the east flank. The outer ward mostly surrounds the inner enclosure, and its construction rendered the massive gatehouse obsolete; a feeble new gateway was built at the rear of the castle overlooking the steep drop to the sea. The walls of this outer enclosure are poorly preserved and only the lower courses survive of two additional rectangular towers set to protect the flank most vulnerable to attack. The most northerly was known as the Engine Tower, and probably held a large crossbow or catapult on the roof to guard the steep road up from the village.

Cricieth has been subjected to more controversy over its building history than any of the castles included in this book, and the arguments over who built what still go on. As can be seen from the plan, the castle falls into two clearly defined stages (the inner and outer wards) and at first everyone was happy to accept the entire structure as Welsh work. Then came the discovery of King Edward's hefty expense bill, which somehow had to be tied in to the existing ruin. Experts therefore suggested that the outer ward was Welsh (because of its similarity to other native sites) and the inner ward was King Edward's work (because of the typically English gatehouse). Current opinion has swung back towards the original interpretation; the inner ward is now believed to have been the primary

A bird's eye reconstruction of Cricieth as it might have looked in the time of Llywelyn the Great. His grandson added an outer enclosure, and Edward I later carried out substantial alterations

structure here built by Llywelyn the Great, and the gatehouse was probably modelled on the one at Henry III's new castle at Montgomery, which Llywelyn would have seen on campaign in 1228. Most, if not all of the outer ward was added by Llywelyn ap Gruffudd, leaving Edward responsible for rebuilding and heightening the main towers following siege damage in 1283.

Access: Cricieth is in the care of CADW and open standard hours. It lies in the village of the same name, on the A497 from Porthmadog to Pwllheli. The ticket office contains an interesting exhibition on the castles of the Welsh Princes, and the travels of Gerald of Wales (OS map ref: SH 500 377).

Cynfal

In 1147 Cadwaladr ap Gruffudd built an earth and timber castle on the tip of a ridge overlooking the Dysynni estuary, in order to consolidate his hold on southern Gwynedd. He placed in charge of it Morfran, abbot of the nearby Celtic religious community at Tywyn – an odd choice it might seem, but that year the redoubtable abbot proved trustworthy to his temporal lord when the sons of Owain Gwynedd decided to raid Cynfael. Relations between Owain and his ambitious brother Cadwaladr had been strained for some time, and so Owain may not have entirely disapproved of the campaign. As the chronicles relate, Morfran refused to hand over the castle, 'though he was tempted at times with threats, at other times with innumerable gifts…for he preferred to die worthily than to lead his life deceitfully'. This only enraged Owain's son, Hywel, who then led a furious assault on the castle, and it was only with difficulty that Morfran escaped alive. The siege of Cynfal was one of the highlights of Hywel's life, and in an elegy to him the poet Cynddelw describes the keep tumbling down, engulfed in flames.

All is peaceful now at Cynfal. Rabbits garrison the gorse-covered mound and there is a splendid view across the broad river valley. Cadwaladr's motte is encircled with a rock-cut ditch, and a rampart around the edge of the mound summit perhaps conceals the remains of a drystone wall. There was probably a tower and other timber buildings within the small courtyard.

Access: the overgrown mound is on private land above Bryn-y-castell farm 3km east of Tywyn, but can be seen from a public footpath starting from Rhyd-yr-onnen station on the Talyllyn railway. From Tywyn take the A493 to Dolgellau, turn right at Bryncrug village for the station (OS map ref: SH 615 016).

Deganwy

According to legend this rugged hill beside the Conwy estuary was the stronghold of the sixth century King Maelgwn Gwynedd, and excavations have uncovered finds of Dark Age and Roman date here. Deganwy guarded an important crossing point on the river, and was the high tide of English advances into native territory. As such, it suffered frequently in the varying fortunes of war. The first castle was built by the Norman Earl Robert of Rhuddlan in 1088, and this was captured and refortified by Llywelyn the Great in 1213. Unfortunately, very little can be identified of Llywelyn's fortress, apart from the base of a round turret and a short length of curtain wall on the larger of the hill's two summits. A stone bracket found during excavations (and now on display at the National Museum of Wales in Cardiff) bears the image of a crowned head – perhaps that of Llywelyn himself. In the turmoil following Llywelyn's death his son and heir Dafydd destroyed the castle before it could be taken by Henry III and used against him; but the king nevertheless reoccupied the site and spent lavish sums on rebuilding the fortress. All this work was in vain, for in 1263 Llywelyn ap Gruffudd starved the garrison into surrender and demolished this hated symbol of royal power so thoroughly that only scattered fragments remain to be seen today. Deganwy never rose again, and when Edward I conquered the Welsh in

1283 he moved the seat of English power to a new site across the river at Conwy.

Access: Freely accessible. The twin peaks of Deganwy hill lie 3km south of Llandudno, close to Conwy, and can be reached by several paths from the A546 (OS map ref: SH 783 795).

Only jagged stumps remain of the Welsh castle on Deganwy hill

The castles of King Edward I

By the second half of the thirteenth century castle building had moved away from the concept of a massively defended strong point (the keep). Most castles had several towers of rounded plan jutting out from the walls, with strategically placed arrow slits to give archers effective covering fire along the defensive line. When King Edward I moved against the Welsh in the wars of 1276-7 and 1282-3 he embarked on a costly building scheme using the most up-to-date defensive trends and the most skilled craftsmen of the time. The king's works in Wales represent the peak of medieval castle design, and more than seven hundred years after they were built, the towering ruins draw visitors from all over the world.

Flint

Rhuddlan

The first to be built was Flint on the Dee estuary (started in 1277), an almost perfect square enclosure with four round corner towers – although one was vastly enlarged like an independently controlled keep. The design of Flint was probably inspired by the fortified town of Aigues Mortes in southern France, visited by Edward in 1270 on his way to the crusades. Further along the coast is Rhuddlan, one of the earliest examples of a concentric castle in Britain where one line of defence lay within another, thus increasing the obstacles facing any attacker. Aberystwyth (built 1277) was another castle of this type, but there is now little left to see. In contrast Conwy (1283) is a collection of huge round towers, clustered

together on a restricted rock above the river estuary. Edward's masons had better luck with Harlech (1283), where the rocky site still allowed the construction of a majestic concentric fortress. The towering inner ward defences completely dwarf the outer line of defence; enabling archers stationed high up to target any attacker with ease. Probably the most famous of the Edwardian castles is Caernarfon (1283), where a pre-existing motte and bailey was encased in a conglomeration of multi-angular towers inspired by the ancient walls of Constantinople.

Caernarfon

Carreg Cennen

As well as the royal fortresses, the king ordered his lords and barons to built castles at their own expense for the defence of the principality. Henry de Lacy built Denbigh in 1283 with its Caernarfon-style multi-angular towers and a unique triple towered gatehouse. John Giffard rebuilt the older Welsh site on the towering crag of Carreg Cennen around 1300, by which time the king had started work on the last major medieval stronghold in Wales – Beaumaris on Anglesey. It was built in the aftermath of an uprising in 1294, and is one of the finest examples of the concentric design in Britain. The high-walled inner ward with its corner towers and two massive gatehouses, sits within a less heavily defended outer ward, the whole being surrounded with a moat accessible by boat from the sea. But as work continued on Beaumaris the threat of a Welsh revolt receded and Edward's last, and greatest monument to his military ambitions, was left unfinished.

Denbigh

Only the site remains of the Welsh fortress at Denbigh, for the huge ruins now crowning the hilltop belong to a later castle started by Earl Henry de Lacy in 1282. Denbigh was another residence of the Welsh Princes; Llywelyn the Great was here in 1230, and his grandson Dafydd ap Gruffudd regarded it as his principal stronghold. After Edward defeated Llywelyn in 1277, Dafydd was left in control of the territory and presumably carried out some rebuilding work. His castle contained a hall, chapel, bakehouse, stores and must have been a fairly substantial building for it withstood the English army for a month in 1282. The present ruin does not seem to incorporate any pre-1282 work and, given Dafydd's rather unique approach to castle building (see Caergwrle), it would be pointless to speculate on the original appearance of Denbigh.

Access: In the care of CADW and open standard hours. The castle lies on the hilltop above Denbigh town in the Vale of Clwyd (OS map ref: SJ 052 657).

Deudraeth

This was the second stone castle mentioned by Gerald of Wales as having been built in 1188 (see Carn Fadryn), and it belonged to Gruffudd and Maredudd ap Cynan, grandsons of Owain Gwynedd, who held this portion of Owain's divided territories. The castle (which is also known as Aber Iâ) was set on a rocky headland between the estuaries of the rivers Dwyryd and Glaslyn, hence the name *deu-draeth* – 'two sands'. Exactly what stood on this natural motte is a puzzle; only a very ruined wall above a rock-cut ditch remains today, but antiquarian accounts imply there was a little round tower on one side of a small enclosure. Also a lost painting suggests there was a keep here. In the nineteenth century a castellated mansion was built nearby and the owner of the estate supposedly demolished the medieval ruin to deter visitors. Time and decay have almost completed the work of man, and the few remains now overlook a playground above Clough Williams-Ellis's fantasy village of Portmeirion.

Access: The site lies in the woods just west of Portmeirion village, on the A487 road between Porthmadog and Penrhyndeudraeth, and is freely accessible subject to admission to the village itself (OS map ref: SH 588 372).

Dinas Emrys

According to legend, this tree-covered rocky hill was the site of Vortigern's Dark Age stronghold, and archaeologists have found evidence of Roman and post-Roman activity here. Traces of the ancient stone walled ramparts remain to be seen, but the most obvious structure on the hill is the base of a rectangular keep. The tower was built sometime in the late-twelfth or early-thirteenth century (possibly by Llywelyn the Great) to guard the mountain road through the valley to the pass of Snowdon. The stones are bonded in clay rather than mortar, so it is hardly surprising that only the lower courses of the basement level have managed to survive to this day.

Access: there is no public access to Dinas Emrys, although the hill borders the A498 road to Capel Curig, 2 km north-east of Beddgelert (OS map ref: SH 606 492).

Dolbadarn

Just as the tower of Dinas Emrys guarded one of the many winding roads crossing the treacherous mountain passes, so Dolbadarn kept watch over another. The little castle is spectacularly overshadowed by the rugged heights of Snowdon, a formidable natural stronghold that effectively kept the English out of Gwynedd until the end of the thirteenth century. Like most of the Welsh castles, very little is known about the history of Dolbadarn. The Tudor antiquarian John Leland was the first to record the tradition that Llywelyn ap Gruffudd imprisoned his brother Owain here for over twenty years after defeating him in battle. Following King Edward's victory, parts of the castle were dismantled and timbers removed to Caernarfon to be used in the new fortress there, a symbolic, as well as a practical measure. However, Dolbadarn still had an administrative role to play as a royal manor, and the castle remained

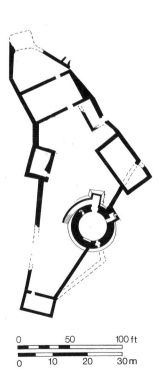

0   50   100 ft
0   10   20   30 m

Dolbadarn Castle

in use into the early-fourteenth century, before it was finally abandoned and left to decay.

The only substantial remaining part of the castle is the grim and dominating round keep, beloved of artists and antiquarians since the dawn of the Romantic movement. Turner painted a memorable image of the tower silhouetted against the misty mountains, with a group of figures (perhaps including the captive Owain) huddled on the shores of Llyn Padarn in the foreground. Historically, the keep was almost certainly built by Llywelyn the Great in the early-thirteenth century, in imitation of the round towers then gaining favour among the English lords in South Wales. The rest of the castle is an insignificant collection of drystone walls arranged haphazardly around the rocky site. A large rectangular hall can be seen, as well as two square towers and the foundations of another building (dating from the English occupation) overlying the line of the demolished curtain wall. Although these defences appear to pre-date the keep, they are probably contemporary and represent the best work the local masons could produce; Llywelyn was only willing to spend his money on specialist builders for the great tower it seems. Originally the walls must have stood about threem high, since there is a first-floor doorway in the keep that led out onto the wall-walk. The only sign of an entrance is a later postern in the east side, but it is possible that the original gateway was in the demolished south curtain wall.

Llywelyn's tower still stands remarkably complete, although the battlements have gone and a modern stone stair replaces the original timber steps. The first-floor entrance was defended with a portcullis and stout wooden door, and led into a large circular room with a fireplace and garderobe. The dark basement store would only have been reached through a trapdoor and ladder in the floor. In contrast to most Welsh towers, Dolbadarn has an additional upper floor, and perhaps it was here that Owain spent his long years of captivity. This was a comfortable room by medieval standards, with whitewashed walls, plenty of windows, a large fireplace, and another garderobe – but a prison is still a prison, and all Owain would have seen from the glassless windows was the bleak, misty slopes of the grey mountains.

Access: In the care of CADW and freely accessible. Dolbadarn lies just outside the village of Llanberis on the A4086 Caernarfon to Betws-y-coed road (OS map ref: SH 586 597).

Dolforwyn

For many years this large castle lay shrouded under layers of grass and rubble and only now, after painstaking excavations and consolidation work, has the plan been fully revealed. Dolforwyn ('maiden's meadow') was begun in 1273 by Llywelyn ap Gruffudd as much of a snub to royal authority as a border stronghold of his expanded dominions. The Prince needed to consolidate his hold on southern Powys in order to demonstrate his authority over the untrustworthy Gruffudd ap Gwenwynwyn, and

This bird's-eye reconstruction shows Dolforwyn castle as it would have appeared around 1276, based on evidence uncovered in recent excavations. The three main towers (of varying shape) can be seen, along with the hall block and a deep well

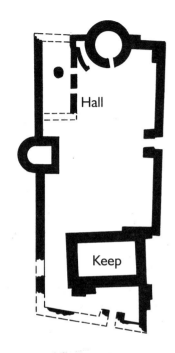

Hall

Keep

0   50   100 ft

0   10   20   30 m

check the growing strength of the Marcher lord Roger Mortimer. He even established a small town beside the castle to bring some measure of economic stability to the area. The newly crowned King Edward I had yet to return to England from the crusades, and in his absence officials attempted to ease fears among the neighbouring lords by forbidding Llywelyn to continue with his scheme. In a haughty reply, Llywelyn wrote that the rights of his principality were entirely separate from those of the king's realm, and that the Welsh had the right to build castles in their own lands without obstruction from anyone.

But the new castle's threat to the royal power base at nearby Montgomery could not be ignored for long. When the English moved against Llywelyn in the war of 1276, Dolforwyn was swiftly besieged by Mortimer and the Earl of Lincoln, Henry de Lacy. After the garrison surrendered Mortimer placed the king's anglophile ally, Gruffudd ap Gwenwynwyn in charge of the site. The castle remained occupied for some years, but the breezy hilltop location was never conducive to urban growth, and Mortimer encouraged the development of a new settlement (unsurprisingly called Newtown) on the banks of the Severn a few kilometres away. Dolforwyn was neglected and left to decay, and by the end of the fourteenth century it was said to be ruinous.

In plan the castle consists of a long rectangular enclosure with a large oblong keep at the front end, a round tower at the opposite end, and an apsidal tower jutting out of the flanking wall on one side. Rock-cut ditches at either end of the ridge isolated the castle site from attack. There were two typically feeble Welsh gateways, and several buildings ranged against the inner walls (although most belong to the period of English occupation). The basement of an early hall block can be identified in the northern corner, with a central mass of masonry that once supported a hearth warming the first-floor chamber. The inner courtyard was divided in two by another ditch crossed by a stone arched bridge, and there is a deep well beside the apsidal tower. According to a survey drawn up in 1322 the buildings within the castle included a chapel, hall, Lady's Chamber, kitchen, granaries, brewery and bakehouse. Not all of these can be identified with the existing ruins, but

Dolforwyn: a view of the excavated foundations of the hall

the latter must be the building alongside the keep with a cluster of domed ovens in the corner. On the hilltop beyond the outer ditch can be seen low earthworks that mark the site of Llywelyn's ill-fated town.

Dolforwyn displays a number of archaic features typical of native building styles, particularly the basic gateways and awkward corners susceptible to undermining. Indeed, for such a late castle, it is very simple affair and indicates how little things had progressed among the Welsh architects. Llywelyn would certainly have seen the effective new fortifications being built by his enemies (particularly Gilbert de Clare, who relied on water-filled moats, round towers and multiple lines of defence to defend his new castle at Caerphilly, which Llywelyn had attacked only a few years previously). Here at Dolforwyn the main strength of the castle is its location on a steep, and relatively inaccessible hilltop. One interesting fact revealed by excavation is that the keep and round tower are not bonded into the curtain walls, indicating they were built first as freestanding structures. The English complaints of 1273 forbid Llywelyn to

Welsh abbeys and monasteries

Strata Florida Abbey

Military might and religious fervour went hand in hand in the Middle Ages. Bloodthirsty warlords would endow religious establishments for the good of their souls, as a sort of insurance policy for the next life. During the twelfth century abbeys and monasteries sprang up throughout Britain, their noble buildings financed by land grants and monetary contributions from wealthy benefactors. At first the Welsh rulers viewed the more orthodox religious organisations with suspicion and preferred the homegrown Celtic monasticism, which had developed in the Dark Ages. But during the course of the century the Cistercian order made headway in Wales and inspired the princes with their austere lifestyles. The 'white monks' favoured remote locations to establish a monastery, away from any distractions to a contemplative lifestyle and where bleak wastes could be turned into productive land.

The first Cistercian House in Wales was founded in 1143 at Cwm-hir in Powys. Warfare brought the early venture to an abrupt end, and the community had to be re-established 33 years later. A similar shaky start afflicted the most famous of all native monasteries, **Strata Florida** or Ystrad Fflur ('the vale of flowers'), which was

Abbey Cwm-Hir

re-founded by the Lord Rhys in 1184. So closely was the abbey linked with the Welsh leaders that King John even contemplated its destruction in 1212. Here the *Brut y Tywysogion* was written, political meetings convened and princes buried in splendour.

However, the Welsh monasteries were never as wealthy as those in Norman England, and none of the princes had enough money to fund lavish building schemes. **Abbey Cwm-hir** (founded 1176), **Talley** (1189), and **Cymer** (1198) had their building plans severely curtailed. The nave at Cwm-hir was an immense 73m long (the same as Canterbury Cathedral), but there is little evidence that the building was ever completed. It was to here that Llywelyn ap Gruffudd's body was brought for burial in 1282. Perhaps the grandest of all the Welsh monasteries is **Valle Crucis** near Llangollen, which was founded in 1201 by Madog ap Gruffudd in a tranquil valley beneath the hilltop fortress of Dinas Brân. On Anglesey Llywelyn Fawr reorganised the ancient Celtic church at **Penmon** as an Augustinian priory. The austere building is still used for worship today since it was taken over as a parish church at the Reformation; sadly the majority of Welsh monastic houses fell victim to the iconoclastic reforms of Henry VIII and now lie in ruins.

Valle Crucis Abbey

Penmon Priory

'repair and construct' the castle, which might suggest that there was already something standing here, perhaps an unfinished fortress started at an earlier date by the rulers of Powys. There is also a rounded knoll on the ridge beyond the round tower, which looks very much like a worn-down motte, although it could alternatively be a temporary earthwork constructed during the siege of 1276-77.

Access: In the care of CADW and freely accessible. Dolforwyn lies 6km north-east of Newtown, off the A483 to Welshpool. After crossing the river by Abermule, take the left turn to Dolforwyn Hall, then next left, and continue up the hill to a small parking area. From here a steep footpath leads up to the castle (OS map ref: SO 153 950).

Dolwyddelan

From a rocky eyrie overlooking the Lledr valley, Dolwyddelan is perhaps the most impressive of the native castles of North Wales, and the restored walls give a good impression of what these towers looked like in their prime. The earliest fortification here was Tomen Castell, a natural rocky knoll with the shapeless ruin of a stone keep on the summit. This lies down in the valley near the river, and it was probably here that Llywelyn the Great was born around 1173. His childhood was spent in Powys away from his murderous relatives at court, but when he gained power Llywelyn ordered the rebuilding of his birthplace as a small, but strong castle to guard the mountain pass.

Ditches were cut through the rock, isolating a natural mound, and on the highest part was raised a two storey oblong tower. As with other Welsh keeps, the main chamber was on the first floor over a dark basement, and was reached by an external flight of steps leading into a defensible porch or forebuilding. The solitary living room has a fireplace and garderobe built into in the thick walls. Another wall passage contains a stair rising to the battlements. The adjoining courtyard was encircled with a low curtain wall of slightly later date, and entered through the usual weak gateway. Towards the end of the thirteenth century a second tower was constructed in the opposite corner of the courtyard – this is usually attributed to Edward I, although the

rather spartan details suggest Llywelyn ap Gruffudd was responsible, and it does resemble his work at Cricieth. There must have been some building here before (perhaps a timber-framed hall) because there is a garderobe in one corner. The English took possession of Dolwyddelan in January 1283, and royal accounts mention the interesting detail that white cloth was supplied to the garrison, so that the soldiers could make camouflage wear for winter patrols in the mountains. At the end of the fifteenth century the derelict castle was briefly reoccupied by a local nobleman, Maredudd ap Ieuan, who added an extra floor to the keep. Thereafter it was abandoned and left to decay. In the nineteenth century the ruined keep was heavily restored when new floors and a roof was added.

Access: In the care of CADW and open standard hours. Dolwyddelan lies 8 km north of Blaenau Ffestiniog on the A470 to Betws-y-coed (OS map ref: SH 721 523).

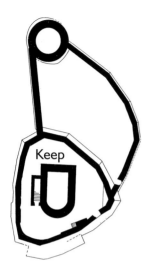

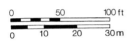

Ewloe Castle

Ewloe

Do not go to Ewloe expecting to see a towering ruin dominating the surrounding landscape, for unlike most native sites, this castle lies unobtrusively tucked away on a wooded hillside above the Dee estuary. The only historical reference to Ewloe appears in a document of 1311 where it is retrospectively mentioned that Llywelyn ap Gruffudd 'built a castle in the corner of the wood' in 1257. The prince had then just defeated his siblings in battle and was embarking on a reconquest of native territories in North Wales. Ewloe was therefore positioned to face east, towards England and the coast road from Chester, rather than looking back into Welsh-held lands. This may explain the odd location of the little fortress.

A very deep rock-cut ditch protects the vulnerable uphill flank and isolates a rounded platform on which was built an apsidal keep. This is now the most prominent part of the ruins and at first glance appears largely intact, but in fact most of the rear wall has gone, providing visitors with a 'cross-section' view. The interior of the keep was divided into a dark basement store, with a main first-floor apartment reached by an outside stairway. There was no fireplace here, but heating was provided by a hearth supported on the timber floor by a stone pillar rising from the basement. On the remaining wall can be seen the outline of the steeply pitched roof, as well as a line of holes that once supported the beams of an external fighting gallery.

The keep was surrounded by a low stone curtain wall extending down the sides of the mound as a revetment, to reinforce the natural bedrock and hinder any attempts at undermining. The simple gateway was accessed via a timber bridge across the surrounding ditch. Another bridge led into the larger lower ward, which would have contained other domestic and ancillary buildings and was defended by a two-storey round tower at the further end.

Some historians have taken the documented building date of 1257 at face value and consider the castle to be solely the work of Llywelyn ap Gruffudd; others think it was built in stages and perhaps started by Llywelyn the Great. Certainly the apsidal keep is comparable to the latter's work at Carndochan

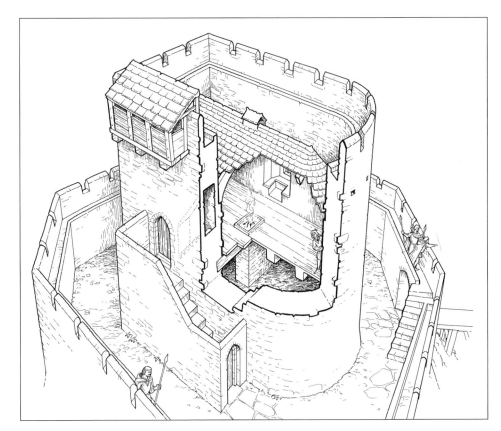

Cutaway view through the apsidal keep at Ewloe. Like other Welsh towers there was only one habitable chamber over a dark basement. Stairs in the thick walls led up to the battlements

and Castell y Bere, and there are at least two discernable building phases here, represented by the primary upper ward and the added lower ward (though whether this was due to a gap of several generations or just a few years, is impossible to say). This hypothesis is confirmed by the separate access into each courtyard – an unnecessary duplication and defensive weakness if the castle was designed in a single scheme. It has even been suggested that the rounded layout of the upper ward reflects the existence of an older motte castle.

The end of Ewloe is just as uncertain as its beginning. When King Edward moved against the Welsh in 1276 the castle was probably abandoned, perhaps even wrecked by the retreating garrison, and with the building of nearby Flint castle the diminutive Ewloe was rendered superfluous and left to decay.

Access: In the care of CADW and freely accessible. The castle lies in woods beside the B5125 Northop to Hawarden road, 1.5km west of Ewloe village. From the lay-by there is a short walk across a field (OS map ref: SJ 288 675).

Llanrhystud

In the Welsh uprisings following the death of Henry I, Owain Gwynedd seized the realm of Ceredigion and allowed his brother Cadwaladr to build a castle at Llanrhystud in 1149 in an effort to stabilise the territorial gains. Unfortunately, the enmity that festered between the family members soon brought about an end to this venture. Owain's son Hywel had already attacked and destroyed his uncle's castle at Cynfal, and now he turned his attention to Llanrhystud. In 1150 Hywel took over the castle for himself, but lost it the following year to the rightful rulers of Ceredigion. The young Lord Rhys of Deheubarth and his brothers captured the castle 'after a long siege' according to the chronicles; but the spiteful Hywel returned a few months later, slaughtered the garrison, and razed the timber defences to the ground. It must have been rebuilt, for Llanrhystud makes a final appearance in the chronicles in 1158 when it was captured by the Normans. A short time later Rhys retaliated and burned all the English-held castles in Ceredigion, presumably bringing the life of this contested fortress to an end.

Cadwaladr's castle is the ringwork known as Caer Penrhos, situated on a lofty hilltop overlooking the Cardiganshire coast, and consisting of a small courtyard enclosed by a massive rampart and outer ditch. A gap through the bank marks the position of the entrance. This ringwork straddles the line of a much larger outer enclosure, which could be an abnormally large bailey or (more probably) a re-used Iron Age hillfort.

Access: Caer Penrhos lies on private land on the hilltop just east of Llanrhystud village, on the A487 between Aberaeron and Aberystwyth. The earthworks can just be seen from a minor road to Llangwyryfon (OS map ref: SN 552 695).

Pen y Castell

High on a rocky outcrop overlooking the Conwy valley is the ruinous remains of a small stone fortification. The whole site is now very overgrown, but it is still possible to identify a series of drystone walls and revetments enhancing the natural slopes and outcrops. The entrance seems to have been at the southern end of this elongated ridge and led through two courtyards or baileys separated by a rock-cut ditch. At the highest part of the site is a roughly circular enclosure with drystone walls up to 3m thick and still standing over 2m high in places. There are no obvious traces of any internal buildings, but perhaps originally there were timber lean-to structures against the inner walls.

Pen y castell has no recorded history and its age is unknown, but the site is too compact and well built to be anything other than a native medieval stronghold. The primitive layout suggests a date in the twelfth century or earlier. Like Carn Fadryn and Castell Prysor, this seems to be an attempt to create a Norman-style fortification using traditional Welsh skills and materials, resulting in a curious hybrid that basically resembles a ringwork and bailey.

Access: the site lies on an overgrown ridge above the A470 about 4 km north of Llanrwst, but is not particularly easy to find. At Maenan Abbey Hotel, turn off the main road and head uphill to a signposted car park for the National Trust owned Cadair Goch viewpoint. From here follow the path through the woods and up the hill; where it levels off double back and follow the crest of the ridge to the site (SH 793 667).

Tomen y Rhodwydd

This fine motte and bailey castle is one of many twelfth century earthworks along the Welsh Marches, and is very likely the 'castle in Iâl' mentioned in the chronicles as having been built by Owain Gwynedd in 1149. Owain had seized this chunk of Powys in a bid to expand his territories, but in 1157 suffered a setback at the hands of Henry II, thereby allowing a neighbouring Welsh lord to burn the castle and reclaim the land. In 1212 King John ordered the rebuilding and repair of the 'Castle of Yale', but some experts think this is a reference to another motte at nearby Llanarmon, which was the administrative centre of the territory.

The well-preserved earthworks of Tomen y Rhodwydd can clearly be seen from the roadside, and consist of a low motte with an adjoining oval bailey. The earthworks of the bailey are relatively massive compared to the rather feeble mound, and archaeologists have postulated an intriguing theory to explain this. It is thought that the motte was completed first, and when the builders set about digging the bailey they couldn't use the surplus earth to enlarge and heighten the mound because the wooden keep was already standing on top; therefore the rubble was used to strengthen the outer defences.

Access: on private land but easily seen from the roadside. The castle lies in a field beside the A525 from Wrexham to Ruthin, about 2 km beyond Llandegla village (OS map ref: SJ 177 516).

Lesser castles and lost sites

Apart from the castles described above which can be identified (either by their architecture or historical documentation) to be of Welsh origin, there exist a number of lesser sites that deserve to be mentioned here. Of the hundreds of earth and timber castles in Wales only a fraction have any recorded history, and might therefore have been built by either the Welsh or English. During the Middle Ages the varying tides of war brought territories under the sway of native princes and Norman lords alike, and therefore the origins of the castles in those territories is questionable. The majority are undoubtedly Norman, but it is worth recording the following additional sites that have been identified by some historians as possible native strongholds.

Abergwyngregyn & Caernarfon

Although these two motte and bailey castles were used by the Welsh princes, they were probably built by the Normans in the late-eleventh century during a short-lived invasion of Gwynedd. The mound at Caernarfon *(SH 478 626)* has been absorbed into the huge fortress built by Edward I, while the motte at Abergwyngregyn *(SH 656 726)* can still be seen in the village. Aber was an important court of the princes of Gwynedd, and excavations in 1993 uncovered the foundations of a substantial three-roomed hall at the foot of the mound.

Castell Brynamlwg, Kerry

A remote site on the Shropshire border now reduced to earthworks and buried masonry. It was originally a twelfth century Norman ringwork but was later rebuilt in stone. The castle came under the control of Llywelyn ap Gruffudd from 1267 to 1276, when the gatehouse and two D-shaped flanking towers could have been added. Alternately these were built after the castle was regained by the Fitz Alans of Clun *(SO 167 846)*.

Castell Coch, Ystradfellte

On a narrow and steep-sided ridge between two streams lie the ruinous remains of a small masonry castle. Heaps of mossy red stones outline a simple pentagonal enclosure with a gateway at one corner, and a round tower at the forward point. A great heap of tumbled masonry in the centre of the courtyard marks the remains of a substantial oblong keep. There is a large outer bailey on the level northern approach, defended by a rampart and ditch of massive proportions. This has been considered a native castle built by Llywelyn ap Gruffudd between 1267 and 1276, when his dominions included most of Breconshire. Certainly the plan and remote setting are typically Welsh, but a castle at Ystradfellte is recorded as belonging to William de Braose in the early-thirteenth century, and therefore it could have been built as a fortified hunting lodge for the vast expanse of the Brecon Beacons (SN 936 144).

Corwen

The medieval chronicle *Brenhinedd y Saesson* recorded the building of a castle at Corwen by Owain Gwynedd in 1165. There are several mottes in the area, but it is equally possible that Owain merely refurbished the large Norman mound at Rûg.

Ednyfed's castle

Ednyfed Fychan was chief advisor to Llywelyn the Great, and is said to have had a castle at his manor of Rhos-on-Sea near Llandudno. Several candidates have been put forward including a stone walled fortification of Dark Age date within Bryn Euryn hillfort, and an overgrown and worn-down mound close to the nature reserve car park. Nearby Llys Euryn is not a castle but a ruined late-medieval manor house.

Llywelyn's castle

The only historical reference to this unlocated site appears in the Battle Abbey Chronicle, where it is fleetingly mentioned that Llywelyn ap Gruffudd's 'new castle beyond Brecon' was captured and destroyed by Prince Edward in 1265. This may be a reference to Castell Du (see under 'Castles of the Lesser Dynasties'), or else a large motte at Cwm Camlais in the mountains above Sennybridge (SN 956 261), which has the foundations of a round keep on the summit.

Plas Crug, Aberystwyth

This vanished building on the outskirts of Aberystwyth looked like a typical Welsh square keep with an adjoining courtyard. It might have been the work of Llywelyn the Great when he occupied this area in 1208, but most authorities now dismiss Plas Crug as an eighteenth century folly.

Castles of the Princes of Deheubarth

Aberdyfi

In 1156 Owain Gwynedd attempted to seize territory belonging to the Lord Rhys ap Gruffudd, and he marched with an army south to the Dyfi estuary. There he was met by Rhys, who 'raised a ditch to give battle' as the chronicles relate. The event did not develop beyond a show of strength and after Owain returned home Rhys safeguarded the area by replacing his temporary fortification with a small castle. This is probably the motte known as Domen Las, which lies on a low ridge bordering the rivers Dyfi and Einion. The 'castle of the Dyfi' was captured by the Normans in 1158 and is mentioned no more in records (although subsequent references to Abereinion may in fact relate to this site – see 'lesser castles and lost sites').

Access: the castle is on private land 8 km south-west of Machynlleth, close to the A487 to Aberystwyth. The tree covered mound can be seen on the riverbank between Glandyfi and Voelas (SN 686 969).

Cardigan

Although this strategic fortress was a twelfth century Norman foundation, it is included here as the first recorded masonry castle built by the Welsh. When Cardigan was captured by the Lord Rhys he rebuilt it 'in stone and mortar' in 1171 and it became his most important stronghold, eclipsing even the ancestral base at Dinefwr. During the Christmas festival of 1176 Rhys held a great contest here between musicians and poets – a forerunner of the present day Eisteddfod. But this cultural triumph marked the apogee of the Welsh castle, and Cardigan soon became a pawn in the destructive rivalry between Rhys's heirs. Maelgwn ousted his brother Gruffudd from his lands, and sold the castle to King John for a paltry sum. As Gerald of Wales sadly observed, 'it is remarkable that brothers show more affection to one another when dead, than when living'. The English kings embarked on an extensive rebuilding programme in subsequent years, and it is doubtful any Welsh work remains here now. Even the later medieval buildings barely survived being swallowed up in a Georgian mansion subsequently built on the site. Cardigan castle has been neglected and overgrown for many years, but some restoration work is planned for the future.

Access: the castle has recently been taken over by the Local Authority, but it will be some time before the remains are made safe and public access allowed (SN 177 459).

Carreg Cennen

This stunning ruin perched on the edge of a cliff is not the work of any Welsh prince – none had the wealth or means to build such a powerful fortress – for this is a native site completely reconstructed by the English around 1300. What the earlier Welsh fortress looked like is anyone's guess, but the fact that it was wholly rebuilt (unlike nearby Dinefwr and Dryslwyn which were merely repaired) suggests that it was not very substantial, and relied on the natural strength of the precipitous site. There was a castle here from at least 1248 when the owner, Rhys Fychan, managed to recover it from the English after his own mother had handed it over! Rhys was equally unpopular with his uncle Maredudd of Dryslwyn, who managed to seize Carreg Cennen with Llywelyn's help in 1257. King Edward's forces occupied the castle in 1277 but lost it briefly to the Welsh in 1283 and again in 1287. Thereafter it was completely rebuilt, bringing the history of Carreg Cennen as a native fortress to an end.

Access: in the care of CADW and open standard hours. The castle lies near the village of Trapp, 5 km south-east of Llandeilo off the A483 Ammanford road (SN 667 191).

Dinefwr

Restoration work by CADW has been progressing for years at Dinefwr and this once poorly understood and overgrown castle is now largely accessible to the public. Dinefwr occupies a prominent place in the history of Deheubarth and is traditionally the site of a royal court extending back to the days of Rhodri Mawr and Hywel Dda. Recent excavations have uncovered the remains of two Roman forts close by, but whether there is a Dark Age settlement under the existing ruin is debatable; some authorities have cast doubts on the ancient origins of the castle and view the literary evidence as little more than an attempt to boost the prestige of the Lord Rhys ap Gruffudd.

Dinefwr only makes regular appearances in the chronicles in the thirteenth century when the castle (along with the neighbouring strongholds of Carreg Cennen and Dryslwyn), was caught up in the interminable conflicts that shattered the unity of Deheubarth. The castle passed under the control of Rhys Gryg and his heirs, though not without a fight from other family members. There is an account of a dramatic siege by Rhys Ieuanc in 1213, which is worth quoting in full since it shows the attack methods used by the Welsh at that time. 'And on the first assault the whole castle was taken, except for the tower. And in that all the garrison gathered together and they defended strongly with missiles and stones...and from without archers and crossbow-men were shooting missiles, and sappers digging, and armed knights making unbearable assaults, till they were forced before the afternoon to surrender the tower'. Presumably this tower was an early stone keep since it was able to withstand the initial attack and there is no mention of it being burnt.

It was to end such divisive conflicts that Llywelyn the Great convened a meeting of the Welsh lords in 1216 to apportion the contested territories of the late Lord Rhys, and Dinefwr was ceded to his son Rhys Gryg. However, in 1220 Rhys was forced to render the castle indefensible to satisfy Llywelyn, who had no desire to see any lesser lords gain too much power. When he eventually made his peace with the prince, Rhys was allowed to rebuild Dinefwr and much of what survives today must belong to that period.

When Rhys died in 1233 his inheritance was divided between his sons;

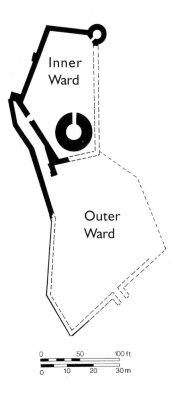

Inner Ward

Outer Ward

0   50   100 ft

0   10   20   30 m

Dryslwyn passed to Maredudd, and Rhys Mechyll received Carreg Cennen and Dinefwr. Maredudd however, was not satisfied with his lot and made strenuous efforts to claim Dinefwr as well, either by enlisting the help of Llywelyn ap Gruffudd, or foolishly conspiring with the English (which resulted in a brief imprisonment for treason); but his efforts were ultimately futile. In 1276 King Edward moved against the Welsh and Maredudd's heir, Rhys, threw in his lot with the English and helped the army take Dinefwr. If Rhys ap Maredudd was expecting the castle as a juicy reward for his aid, then he must have been bitterly disappointed when it was retained by the Crown. The story of Dinefwr as a Welsh stronghold now comes to an end, although the castle continued to be occupied and repaired for many years before it was eventually abandoned in the fifteenth century.

Dinefwr: the top floor of the round keep is a summerhouse added at a much later date

Happily ever after?

Few aristocrats ever married for love; political alliances, social advantages, and monetary gain were the factors that mattered in medieval matrimony. Around 1100 the beautiful princess Nest, daughter of the last king of Deheubarth, married Gerald of Windsor, one of the freebooters busy turning her ancestral lands into a Norman dominion. Together they founded an important dynasty centred on Gerald's newly acquired stronghold at Pembroke. One of her sons became Bishop of St David's, and her grandson was the famous cleric and writer Gerald of Wales.

Nest's beauty was legendary. Would-be admirers lurked for days in the bushes around her home just to catch a glimpse of her face. King Henry I was so smitten that he fathered an illegitimate child with the 'Helen of Wales'. Owain ap Cadwgan, son of the prince of Powys, was also smitten in a big way. The chronicles relate how he was so 'moved with passion and love' for Nest that he broke into Gerald's castle and kidnapped her. In the confusion of the raid, Nest advised her husband to escape down the privy drains, and while Gerald slithered away, Nest remained behind to be taken prisoner (not unwillingly as the story goes). She was soon reunited with her

Dinefwr castle is sited on the highest and most secure part of a steep sided ridge above the Tywi valley, and is surrounded on three sides by deep ditches. The plan suggests the former existence of a ringwork and bailey, but only excavation will confirm if there was anything earlier than the medieval period here. Masonry walls were built around both enclosures, although the irregularly shaped outer ward is now very ruinous. A modern path leads across the inner rock-cut ditch (which has been enlarged by later quarrying) past the middle gateway and into a bottleneck passage that acted as a killing ground for would-be attackers. The inner gate was a simple archway (later reduced in size) leading into the pentagonal-shaped enclosure of the primary inner ward. Here the masonry remains are quite impressive, and their survival

family, and the lusty Owain got his comeuppance several years later, when Gerald arranged his murder in an ambush.

In the following century another politically motivated marriage had a similar tragic conclusion. In 1205 Llywelyn the Great tied the knot with Joan (Siwan), daughter of King John. She was a valuable intermediary between her husband and her father during their strained political relationship, but while Llywelyn was off busy fighting his wars, an illicit romance sprang up between Joan and William de Braose. William had been captured by the Welsh in battle, but became almost an ally of the prince and contracted a marriage between his own daughter and Llywelyn's son Dafydd. But then rumours of the affair reached Llywelyn's ears, and he reacted with understandable fury. Joan was imprisoned for two years and William was hanged from a tree.

Llywelyn eventually forgave his wife and they remained married until her death in 1237. She was buried at Llanfaes on Anglesey, where Llywelyn founded a Franciscan Friary. At the Dissolution of the Monasteries her tomb was removed to Beaumaris church, where the richly decorated stone coffin lid can still be seen.

is due not only to the long years of military use, but also to restoration work carried out when the ruined castle was utilised as an ornamental feature in the landscaped grounds of nearby Newton House.

The inner courtyard is devoid of the stone and timber-framed buildings that once jostled for space, and the principal feature here is a large round keep built by Rhys Gryg sometime between 1220 and 1233. This is clearly modelled on the cylindrical towers then fashionable amongst the Marcher lords, and would have contained two residential chambers above a basement store. A later door has been cut through to the gloomy basement and from inside you can look up and see the outlines of blocked-up doors and windows on the residential upper level. In the eighteenth century the overall appearance of the tower was drastically altered when it was reduced in height and a summerhouse added to the top, which is reached from the battlements across a stone bridge. The much-repaired curtain walls appear to pre-date the keep, and could possibly belong to the reign of Lord Rhys. Small towers of square and round plan were added to strengthen two of the more exposed corners of the enclosure, and after the English took over Dinefwr, a large suite of domestic apartments was added to the north side of the courtyard overlying the demolished curtain wall.

Access: in the care of CADW and open at regular times (but advisable to check in advance). Dinefwr can be reached by a footpath through Castle Woods nature reserve from the bridge below Llandeilo town, or from the grounds of the National Trust owned Newton House, just over a mile west of the town, off the A40 to Carmarthen (SN 611 217).

Dryslwyn

The dramatic ruins of Dryslwyn castle crown the summit of an isolated steep-sided hill in the Tywi valley, just a few miles away from the main Welsh stronghold at Dinefwr. Both sites are closely connected historically and are said to occupy the site of ancient hillforts (although in truth there is little evidence to back up the claim). This is a large and substantial castle, and yet Dryslwyn hardly makes an appearance in the chronicles before the English captured it in 1287. The earliest reference is to a siege here in 1246, but the outcome is unfortunately not recorded. Recent excavations have proved that part of the castle had been built some years before, probably in the early-thirteenth century by Rhys Gryg, the Lord of Dinefwr. On the highest part of the hill Rhys built a round keep with an adjoining inner ward of irregular plan, which was entered through a simple gateway beside the tower. The overall plan closely resembles his work at Dinefwr. Within the sloping courtyard stood an oblong block containing a basement store with a large hall above, and also a small prison and detached kitchen. The inner ward appears to have been defended by an earthwork outer bailey curving around the

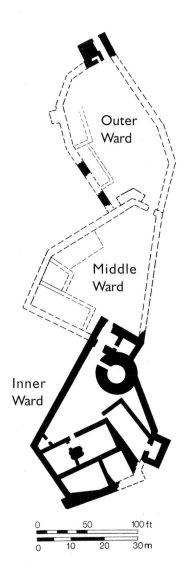

Outer Ward

Middle Ward

Inner Ward

0   50   100 ft

0   10   20   30 m

more vulnerable northern flank of the hilltop.

After Rhys died the castle passed to his son Maredudd, who added another hall and strengthened the defences by rebuilding part of the outer ward in stone. The next lord of Dryslwyn, Rhys ap Maredudd, was stubbornly opposed to Prince Llywelyn and had sided with the king during the wars of 1276-77 and 1282-83. His loyalty was duly rewarded and the revenues from his new lands financed the next phase of the castle's development. Rhys rebuilt the southern side of the inner ward and added a small square chapel tower overlooking the steep drop to the river. The courtyard was practically filled up with domestic buildings and the approach to the castle was further strengthened by the addition of a third ward with a projecting square gatetower. These extensions turned

Dryslwyn into the largest Welsh fortress ever built. Rhys even encouraged the growth of a small town outside the gates – but all this work was soon to end in disaster. Though initially loyal to the king, Rhys began to resent and fear the continual interference of royal administrators and in 1287 lashed out in revolt. The Crown took the rebellion seriously and a huge army was quickly assembled to lay siege to the castle throughout the summer months. A large stone-throwing machine was used to breach the walls, while miners dug a collapsible tunnel under the defences. This was a tried and tested method

Excavated foundations of the round keep at Dryslwyn

of bringing down walls, but the tunnel collapsed prematurely and everyone inside was killed. Despite this dreadful setback, the attacking force managed to break in through the chapel at the beginning of September, although by then the wily Rhys had slipped away to his remaining stronghold at Newcastle Emlyn. The uprising fizzled out, and in 1290 he was captured by disloyal followers and dragged away to a savage execution.

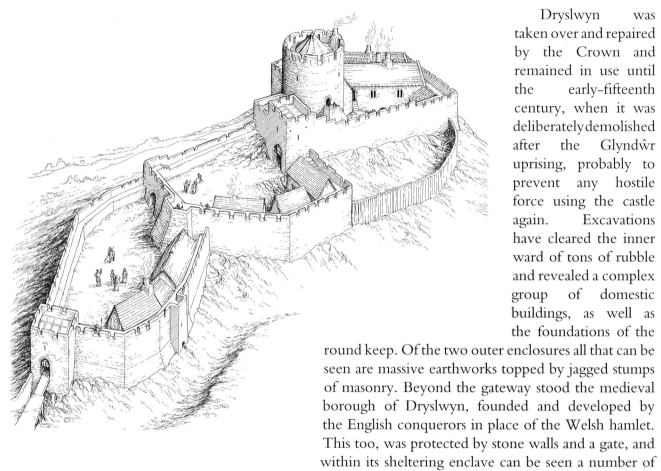

Dryslwyn was taken over and repaired by the Crown and remained in use until the early-fifteenth century, when it was deliberately demolished after the Glyndŵr uprising, probably to prevent any hostile force using the castle again. Excavations have cleared the inner ward of tons of rubble and revealed a complex group of domestic buildings, as well as the foundations of the round keep. Of the two outer enclosures all that can be seen are massive earthworks topped by jagged stumps of masonry. Beyond the gateway stood the medieval borough of Dryslwyn, founded and developed by the English conquerors in place of the Welsh hamlet. This too, was protected by stone walls and a gate, and within its sheltering enclave can be seen a number of platforms and terraces marking the site of long-lost homes.

Access: In the care of CADW and freely accessible. Dryslwyn lies 8 km west of Llandeilo, just off the A40 to Carmarthen. There is a car park at the foot of the hill, from where a path leads up to the ruins (SN 554 204).

Nevern

Nevern was a motte and bailey founded by the Normans in the twelfth century, but is included here as an example of a castle taken and substantially refortified by the Welsh. The original castle appears to have made use of an older Iron Age hillfort, and a small motte was heaped over an angle of the curving outer rampart. At the most secure part of the enclosure (where rocky slopes tumble headlong to the valley below) a deep ditch was cut through the rock, isolating a small inner ward. This was surrounded by a low stone wall with a central square keep of modest proportions. There are traces of a round tower on top of the motte, but this could be later work.

It is possible that the stone defences belong to the time of the Lord Rhys, for he seized Nevern in 1191 from his son-in-law William fitz Martin, despite having sworn an oath to the contrary. Gerald of Wales recounted the story with relish, adding that Rhys himself was imprisoned at the castle a few years later by his rebellious sons Hywel and Maelgwn. Within a few months Hywel repented of his action, turned against his brother and released his father from captivity. After Rhys died in 1197 the power of Deheubarth waned for good and the Welsh withdrew from this outlying territory. The Fitz Martins soon moved back and founded a new power base nearby at Newport.

Access: The castle is freely accessible and lies on the hill above St Brynach's church in the village. Nevern lies 3 km east of Newport, signposted off the A487 road to Cardigan (SN 083 402).

Newcastle Emlyn

Around 1240 King Henry III divided the territory of Emlyn between Maredudd ap Rhys Gryg, and the Earl of Pembroke. The western half was controlled from the Earl's castle of Cilgerran, and so Maredudd built a 'new castle' to defend his part. The castle was built on a site offering good defensive capabilities – a steep-sided ridge within a hairpin bend of the river Teifi. Maredudd's alliance with the King brought him into conflict with the other Welsh lords and in 1259 he was convicted of treason against Llywelyn and imprisoned for a while at Cricieth. When Maredudd died in 1271 his castles of Emlyn and Dryslwyn passed to his son Rhys, who rebelled against the Crown in 1287. The English captured Emlyn, but barely a month after the main rebel base at Dryslwyn was taken, Rhys launched a surprise attack and succeeded in regaining his Teifi-side stronghold. Another large army was assembled to march on Emlyn, and the surviving accounts for this laborious campaign list up to sixty oxen used to haul a great siege machine from Dryslwyn. Hundreds of beach stones were brought along for use as missiles for this fearsome sling to pound the castle into submission.

By the time the army battered their way inside, Rhys had slipped away again and remained at large until 1290. With his execution native rule in Deheubarth came to an end. The New Castle passed to the Crown and a lengthy sequence of repair work commenced in the early-fourteenth century. Most of the surviving masonry (including the prominent twin-towered gatehouse) belongs to this period, and perhaps only the foundations of the inner ward and the earthwork outer enclosure dates from the period of Welsh occupation.

Access: the castle is freely accessible and lies just east of the town of Newcastle Emlyn, 13 km from Cardigan on the A484 to Carmarthen (SN 311 407).

The gatehouse at Newcastle Emlyn

Rhayader

Very little now remains of this castle, apart from a rocky platform overlooking the rapids on the river Wye that gave the town its name (rhaeadr – waterfall). The Lord Rhys built the castle in 1177 during a power struggle for the territory of Gwrtheyrnion in Mid Wales. The chronicles go on to record that Rhys rebuilt his outpost in 1194, either because it had been damaged in an attack or perhaps because the defences were being upgraded with

Reconstruction drawing of the siege of Newcastle Emlyn in 1287. On the left can be seen a typical siege engine (a trebuchet) of the period

masonry. In any event the neighbouring Welsh lords of Maelienydd swiftly razed it. The castle passed under English control for a time, but was retaken and destroyed in 1202. It is unlikely that this strategic site was completely abandoned, but little is known of its subsequent history. Whatever stood here must have deteriorated into a very insignificant ruin by the sixteenth century, because the antiquarian John Leland believed the town had never possessed a castle.

Today all that can be seen of Rhayader castle is a roughly level grassy platform on the edge of the river. The sides are still protected by some deep rock-cut ditches (a typical feature of welsh castles), but the modern town has obliterated any remains on the main landward approach. Although it is possible that the defences were made of wood, there is a tradition of stonework here, and the deep ditches would certainly have provided sufficient building materials. Just across the river in the village of Llansantffraed there is a small motte hemmed in by modern houses. This must have played a role in the all the hubris, but it seems too insignificant and archaic to have been the war-worn castle referred to in the chronicles.

Access: the site of the castle lies close to the church just west of Rhayader town centre, on the A470 road to Llangurig (SN 968 680).

Trefilan

According to the chronicles this motte castle took a relatively long time to build, for it was started by Maelgwn ap Rhys shortly before his death in 1231, and finished by his son two years later. However, the wording in the text is rather ambiguous, and Maelgwn's son could either have 'repaired' or 'completed' the castle. A well-preserved ditch still encircles the steep flat-topped mound, which was presumably surmounted by a wooden keep. For such an old-fashioned castle type this motte apparently remained in use for a long time; A letter dated 1282 mentions an attack on Trefilan by King Edward's ally Rhys ap Maredudd, who freed eighteen prisoners and then 'burned down the house' (presumably the castle).

Access: on private land, but the tree-covered mound can adequately be seen from the road in Trefilan village, just off the A482 mid-way between Lampeter and Aberaeron (SN 549 571).

Ystradmeurig

This is one of a number of castles founded by the Normans around 1110 in the course of an intense, but short-lived invasion of Ceredigion. The castle soon passed into Welsh ownership and became one of the most bitterly fought over strongholds in Deheubarth, changing owners at least four times and being damaged or destroyed in 1137, 1151 and 1193. In 1208 Ystradmeurig was demolished by Maelgwn ap Rhys to prevent it falling into the hands of his enemy Llywelyn the Great. This action brought Maelgwn little profit, for Llywelyn still ousted him from Ceredigion and placed the land in the care of his more pliable kinsmen. This is the last time Ystradmeurig is mentioned in the chronicles – was it abandoned at that time, or was its subsequent history uneventful enough to warrant a mention?

Two castles stand guard here today. One of them is a small motte about a mile from the present village and, since it actually lies in the vale (ystrad) of the river Meurig, then it is probably the original Norman site. The Welsh castle is the larger and stronger earthwork on a low ridge behind the village, which inherited the name of its predecessor. This must have been established here by 1193 because the attacking army had to use siege machines to capture it (which would hardly be necessary for the little motte). This is a difficult site to interpret in advance of any excavations, for it is an unusual earthwork and not all that dissimilar to a small hillfort of Iron Age date. The main defensive feature is a curving bank with an outer ditch, crossing the neck of the ridge and segregating an oval courtyard. Within this is a much slighter rampart that attempts to turn the end of the ridge into a secure inner ward. Within the larger outer enclosure are the overgrown footings of an oblong keep, thought to be the work of Lord Rhys or his sons.

Access: on private land, but visible from the roadside. The village of Ystradmeurig lies 3 km east of Pontrhydfendigaid on the B4343 road from Tregaron to Devil's Bridge (SN 702 675).

Lesser castles and lost sites

Abereinion
According to the Brut y Tywysogion this castle was built by the Lord Rhys in 1169 and rebuilt by Maelgwn in 1206. It could be a reference to the castle of Aberdyfi (which also lies close to the aber of the river Einion), but antiquarian references suggest there used to be another Abereinion site near Llandysul.

Castell Gwynionydd, Llandysul

This large ringwork may have been built by Maelgwn ap Rhys when he was granted the territory of Gwynionydd in 1216, and consists of a strong rampart and ditch segregating part of a steep headland above the Teifi valley. Antiquarian references hint at a vanished keep inside (SN 424 421).

Castell Meurig, Llangadog

This fine motte and bailey is mentioned several times in the early-thirteenth century during the family conflicts of Deheubarth, and may therefore be of Welsh origin. More probably it was an outpost of nearby Norman Llandovery (SN 709 276).

Garth Grugyn

Maelgwn Fychan is the documented builder of this unlocated castle in 1242, and one possible contender is Pen y Castell at Llanilar near Aberystwyth. The summit of the steep hill has been shaped into a strong oval bailey separated by a rock-cut ditch from a low-level lumpy motte – perhaps it was never finished (SN 630 746).

Nant yr Arian, Devil's Bridge

Another lost Welsh castle briefly mentioned in 1213. It could have been a mound destroyed in the nineteenth century.

Castles of the Princes of Powys

Bodyddon

Bodyddon castle was not the only casualty of Llywelyn ap Gruffudd's rise to power, but its destruction by the Prince in 1257 was part of a chain of events that created one of his bitterest enemies. At that time castle was held by Gruffudd ap Gwenwynwyn who, like other members of the royal House of Powys, paid the price for being too closely allied with the English Crown. Llywelyn took the castle along with a large chunk of Gruffudd's territories and then drove him out of Wales. After six years of exile, Gruffudd swallowed his pride and paid Llywelyn homage, and had his property reinstated. His subsequent deceptions and involvement in a plot to kill the prince led to a second exile in England, before King Edward placed him back in charge following Llywelyn's downfall. Bodyddon is believed to be the strongly fortified motte of Tomen-yr-allt, loftily secure on a wooded hilltop above the Fyllon valley. It is not known if there were any masonry buildings here, and the castle probably relied on timber defences supplemented with a deep ditch and outer rampart.

Access: the overgrown earthworks lie on private land 2 km north-west of Llanfyllin, on top of a hill bordering the B4391 to Bala (SJ 126 212).

Castle Caereinion

Beside the parish church in the village of Castle Caereinion is a feeble and shapeless mound that marks the last vestiges of a motte built here by Madog ap Maredudd in 1156. The surrounding churchyard possibly marks the extent of a bailey enclosure. When Henry II tried to conquer Wales once and for all in 1165, Madog's nephew, Owain Cyfeiliog, owned the castle. Owain joined the Welsh alliance against the planned invasion, but when he foolishly renewed his friendship with the king the other princes turned on him and booted him out of his territory. His castle at Tafolwern (see below) was handed over to the Lord Rhys, and Caereinion was given to Madog's son, Owain Fychan. But in an epilogue so typical of those violent times, Owain Cyfeiliog returned with a large English army, destroyed Caereinion and slaughtered the garrison. Owain Fychan apparently never achieved any revenge for that act and, in 1187 he was murdered – possibly at the instigation of Owain Cyfeiliog (who spent the remainder of his days peacefully among the brethren of Strata Marcella abbey).

Access: the worn-down remains of the mound can be seen in the churchyard at Castle Caereinion village, 6 km west of Welshpool off the A458 (SJ 163 054).

Cymer

At the beginning of the twelfth century the Prince of Powys, Cadwgan ap Bleddyn, granted the territory of Cymer to his long-time ally Uchdryd ap Edwin, to hold as a feudal vassal. The Chronicles state that Uchdryd held the

land on condition he prove faithful to the lords of Powys, and help in their defence against any enemies. It appears that Uchdryd remained loyal to his charge until Cadwgan died, and then in 1116 he claimed the territory for himself and built a castle to secure his gains. The lords of Powys could not ignore this act, and two of Cadwgan's heirs led an army into Cymer, drove Uchdryd to flight, burned down the castle and divided the territory up between themselves.

Uchdryd's short-lived castle was built on the hillside overlooking the Mawddach estuary, a location offering stunning views but little in the way of any defensive strength. The castle is a small and feeble motte carved out of a natural ridge, with a low outer bank guarding the uphill approach. In the eighteenth or nineteenth century the mound found a new lease of life when a summerhouse was built on top – which is now ruinous and bears a confusing similarity to a medieval keep!

Access: the castle is on private land 2 km north of Dolgellau, off the signposted road to Llanfachreth. Where the road bends by the telephone box, turn left along a minor road towards Cymer, and after about 1 km the mound and tower can be seen uphill on the right hand side (SH 732 195).

Dinas Brân

The remote and evocative ruins of Castell Dinas Brân crown the summit of a steep hill in the Vale of Llangollen, and it is hardly surprising that this atmospheric site has been identified in medieval literature as the stronghold of Bran, a Celtic deity and keeper of the mystical Grail. The hilltop has been fortified since the Iron Age, but the existing ruins date from the second half of the thirteenth century when the lord of Powys Fadog, Gruffudd Maelor (d.1270), opted to build his stronghold on this lofty peak. Like most of the great Welsh castles, Dinas Brân had a relatively short life, for on the outbreak of war in 1276 it was abandoned and burnt by the garrison before the arrival of King Edward's army.

The Earl of Lincoln inspected the smouldering ruins shortly afterwards and wrote to Edward that he had found 'all the houses of the castle burnt, but the tower and walls...intact'. He urged the King to rebuild Dinas Brân, adding the grandiose statement that 'there is no stronger castle in Wales, nor has England a greater' – but this advice was not heeded. Dinas Brân was among the properties later granted to the Earl of Surrey who was more concerned with building a new castle at Holt, than repairing a damaged stronghold on an inaccessible and windswept height.

Today the walls of the castle are very ruinous but the jagged fragments enable most of the plan to be understood. On the highest part of the hill

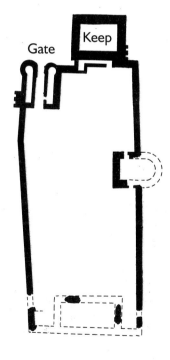

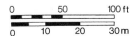

Arms and the man

Heraldry was introduced and developed in England during the twelfth century principally as a means of identification in battle, since knights were clad from head to foot in armour and it was often impossible to distinguish friend from foe. Heraldic devices were emblazoned on surcoats (linen tunics worn over armour) shields, and banners. By the thirteenth century heraldry had developed into a very organised system rigorously maintained by the guild of heralds. They took pleasure in devising arms for legendary figures (such as King Arthur), and creating images to link noble families to their illustrious ancestors. Many of the arms attributed to Welsh rulers were devised as late as Tudor times – such as a version of the crest of the Lord Rhys, depicting the three ravens of Sir Rhys ap Thomas (1449-1525). Those that can be identified as genuinely medieval almost all depict lions, whether upright (*rampant*) or walking (*passant*), in imitation of the royal arms of England. The four-lion crest of Llywelyn ap Gruffudd is attested by contemporary records, and a rampant lion is engraved on the fourteenth century tomb of Lord Rhys at St Davids Cathedral. Owain Gwynedd is credited with having a striking crest of three golden eagles. It is interesting to note that the familiar red dragon (whatever its claims to antiquity) was never borne by the princes of medieval Wales.

the masons built a square keep with a defended forebuilding followed (at a slightly later date) by a large rectangular enclosure. There was an apsidal tower half way along the south wall, and a substantial oblong building (perhaps the hall or another tower) at the furthest end of the courtyard. Two ragged window openings beside the apsidal tower may mark the site of another building (usually identified as a chapel). The whole plan foreshadows the castle Llywelyn ap Gruffudd built at Dolforwyn.

An enormous rock-cut ditch surrounds Dinas Brân on all sides except the east, for here the natural slopes made extra defence unnecessary. The ditch was a formidable obstacle in itself and must have provided the masons with an abundant supply of building materials. An equally monumental timber bridge would have crossed the ditch, providing the only access to the castle. The entrance was squeezed in between the keep and the edge of the hill, and lay between two very narrow and elongated towers. Here can still be seen a few signs of the artistic aspirations of the lords of Powys Fadog; the entrance passage was roofed over with an elaborate rib-vault and some fragments of the original carved stones remain. Perhaps the principal rooms in the castle were similarly decorated, making Dinas Brân one of the most elaborate and impressive status symbols owned by a Welsh prince.

Access: the castle is freely accessible, and can be reached by several steep paths from Llangollen town centre. The easiest way is to drive along a minor road from the A599 from Pontcysyllte to Eglwyseg, and when the hill is reached, take the signposted footpath up to the top (SJ 223 431).

Dinas Brân: ragged walls crown the summit of the hill

Entry to the hilltop fortress of Dinas Brân was guarded by a huge rock-cut ditch, a long timber bridge, and a small gatehouse overlooked by the keep

Tafolwern

When the Prince of Powys, Madog ap Maredudd, died in 1160 his lands were split up amongst his quarrelsome heirs. Owain Gwynedd decided the time was ripe for a bit of land snatching and seized the territory of Cyfeiliog. Two years later a local lord, Hywel ap Ieuaf, captured the principal stronghold in Cyfeiliog, Tafolwern castle. This event coincided with the death of his mother and brought Owain to a very low ebb; 'neither the splendour of sovereignty nor the solace of aught else in the world could win from him his conceived grief' as the chronicles relate. However, after making a raid on Hywel's land and slaughtering his army, Owain soon cheered up and rebuilt the castle.

This event not only shows the strategic importance of Tafolwern, but also implies that Owain Gwynedd was the builder. However, the castle is more likely to have been the work of another Owain – Owain Cyfeiliog – who had been originally granted this territory (and from which he took his nickname) in 1149. This Owain seems to have regained Tafolwern by 1165, but he was stripped of his possessions for renewing allegiance to the English. Tafolwern passed briefly to the Lord Rhys, but with English help Owain Cyfeiliog was reinstated. The last mention of the castle is in 1244, when Owain's grandson, Gruffudd ap Gwenwynwyn, was holed up inside, pleading for English help while being threatened by the army of Dafydd ap Llywelyn. Although the King promised his ally help in the event of an actual siege, the outcome is not recorded and Tafolwern castle is mentioned in the Chronicles no more. All that now remains of this important site is an overgrown motte squeezed into a loop of land between two converging rivers. The mound is not particularly strong, but the rivers make natural moats hampering any direct attack except from the southern approach along the neck of the isthmus. The level ground behind the mound may have been utilised as a bailey.

Access: on private land, but the motte is clearly visible from the roadside just south of Tafolwern village, Llanbrynmair, off the A470 to Dolgellau (SH 891 026).

Welshpool and Powis Castle

'Castell Coch (in English Red Castle), standeth on a rock of dark red coloured stone. It hath two separate wards'; so wrote the succinct and indefatigable antiquarian John Leland around 1540. The great building noted by Leland was then barely three centuries old, but its origins are to be found at the beginning of the twelfth century. The first recorded castle built by the native princes was at Welshpool, and Castell Coch – now more familiarly known as Powis Castle – may well have been the last.

Welshpool motte

In 1111 Cadwgan ap Bleddyn was installed as ruler of Powys by Henry I and came to Welshpool where he decided to build a castle. By the end of the twelfth century southern Powys was ruled by Gwenwynwyn ap Owain Cyfeiliog, whose hostile ambitions provoked an English raid in 1196. After failing to break into the castle with 'diverse engines and siege contrivances' the army sent miners to burrow beneath the ramparts and 'make hidden passages underground'. The castle was eventually captured, and in a rare example of chivalry the defeated garrison was allowed to depart in safety – a compliment repaid to the English soldiers when Gwenwynwyn retook his castle later the same year!

In 1274 Llywelyn ap Gruffudd dispensed with such niceties and razed the fortress to the ground. He had good reason to, for in that year his own brother Dafydd and Gruffudd ap Gwenwynwyn had plotted his assassination. The conspiracy was delayed by bad weather and when the plot leaked out, Llywelyn sent messengers to Welshpool to demand an explanation. Gruffudd courteously provided the messengers with dinner, and then locked them up in the dungeon! In a barefaced act of defiance Gruffudd prepared the castle for war, set up the banner of Powys on the highest tower, and scuttled away to England leaving the garrison to face Llywelyn's wrath. The soldiers wisely surrendered and released the prisoners, whereupon Llywelyn put the castle to the torch.

King Edward reinstated Gruffudd to his lands after the war of 1276-77, and the devious Welshman no doubt derived pleasure from Llywelyn's subsequent downfall and death. After these events the heirs of Gruffudd further ingratiated themselves with the winning side. They were no longer considered Welsh princes but English barons, subject to the king and the laws of the March. The family even adopted the surname 'de la pole' after the place-name (Pool). Gruffudd's son Owain de la Pole probably started to rebuild the war-worn fortress before the estate passed to the Charleton family of Shropshire on the marriage of Owain's daughter Hawys to John de Charleton in 1309. The transition was not as smooth as might be imagined, for Hawys' uncle Gruffudd de la Pole disputed her sole right to possession under English law, and led an attack on the castle. The story of the castle's subsequent history and transformation into a stately home does not concern us here.

A lively debate has sprung up among academics in recent years over the historical development of Welshpool castle, a situation not helped by an abundance of documentary references and the existence of three fortifications in the area! The original foundation of 1111 is probably Domen Castell, a much-altered motte and bailey on the east edge of the town next to the bypass road. A bowling green now occupies the bailey enclosure. Then there is the Lady's Mount motte and bailey in Powis Castle park. A reference to the 'motte of Welshpool' as late as 1299 could relate to either site.

The fact that Llywelyn burned down the castle in 1274 suggests it was still of timber at that date; yet Gruffudd later claimed his gutted stronghold was worth a thousand pounds (a substantial sum in those days), implying that it was a sizeable stone building. Presumably this castle was on the site of the existing mansion, for detailed studies of the upstanding fabric have revealed early masonry remains incorporated into the later structure.

Visitors now approach Powis Castle through the fourteenth-century outer ward, which appears to have replaced an earlier bailey on the opposite side of the rock facing the town. The small and compact inner ward is entered along a narrow passage squeezed between the cheeks of two rounded towers, and now accessed by a grand stone staircase instead of the less welcoming drawbridge and portcullis arrangement of the original fortress. What can be said with some certainty is that this massive twin-towered gatehouse is stylistically unlikely to be earlier than 1300 and quite possibly was built by the Charletons. However, behind this impressive façade is a fragment of an older curtain wall enclosing a circular courtyard on the summit of the rocky hill. This enclosure was subsequently altered by the addition of a hall block and square keep on the sides facing the town. Unfortunately, the extensive rebuilding work that transformed the grim stronghold into a sumptuous mansion with elegant terraced gardens has hampered a fuller understanding of the Welsh castle's origins.

Access: The motte is Welshpool town is now used as a bowling green and can be seen from the roadside if the grounds are closed. Powis Castle and gardens are owned by the National Trust and are usually open to the public from Easter to September (SJ 215 064).

The inner gatehouse of Powis Castle

Lesser castles and lost sites

Kerry

A motte and bailey on the hill beside the village may have been built in the early-twelfth century by Madog ap Idnerth (SO 147 895).

Llanfechain

This very prominent motte and bailey on the outskirts of the village, is thought to have been built by Owain Fychan around 1166 (SJ 294 168).

Oswestry & Castell Brogyntyn

Both these castles lie just outside Wales in Shropshire. The Norman site at Oswestry (SJ 292 298) was rebuilt by Madog ap Maredudd in 1149 during a period of territorial expansion, while the nearby ringwork of Castell Brogyntyn (SJ 274 314) was probably built by his son Owain Brogyntyn (who took the nickname of his stronghold).

Sycharth, Llansilin

One of the most famous of all castle mounds in Wales, Sycharth was the home of Owain Glyndŵr, whose rebellion in 1400 threatened the security of English rule. Although Glyndŵr lived here, the castle was perhaps a twelfth century Norman foundation. His manor house (praised by the court poet Iolo Goch as 'a fine wooden house on the top of a green hill') was razed to the ground by the English in 1403. The earthworks are still prominent today (SJ 205 258).

Castle legends

Myth and history are woven inextricably about the rugged crag of Dinas Emrys in the Gwynant valley. We know that someone (possibly Llywelyn the Great) built an oblong keep on the summit in the Middle Ages, but according to legend the tyrant Vortigern (a real Dark Age ruler) fled here to seek protection from his enemies. He ordered the building of an impregnable tower, but every night the unfinished walls came tumbling down. In desperation his wizards advised him that the only way to make firm the foundations was to seek out a boy who had never had a father, and sprinkle the mortar with his blood. After a lengthy search Vortigern's agents came across young Ambrosius (the 'Emrys' of the place-name) and brought him to the rock. But Ambrosius was smarter than his captors and revealed the real reason why the tower could not be built; beneath the foundations was a pool in which two dragons continually fought, the red dragon symbolising the Welsh, and the white one the invading Saxons. This story was set down by the monk Nennius in the ninth century, but around 1130 Geoffrey of Monmouth published his famous book *The History of the Kings of Britain*, where the character of Ambrosius was rewritten as Merlin.

Another Welsh castle associated with Arthurian legend is Dinas Brân near Llangollen, which has been linked to the Grail castle of the Medieval Romances. The thirteenth century story of *Fouke Fitz Warin* is set in the Welsh Marches and refers to a 'Chastiel Bran', a ruined castle so perilous to enter that only one knight ever escaped alive. But the name Bran has also been connected to the Celtic deity-figure in *The Mabinogion*, who owned a mystical cauldron of rebirth. Perhaps this ancient site was considered by the unknown troubadours to be the perfect setting for their tales of magical events.

The rock of Deganwy near Llandudno is another Dark Age site connected with a historical ruler. Maelgwn Gwynedd ruled north-west Wales from his stronghold above the Conwy. He died around 547 of a plague, but the story goes that the bard Taliesin warned him that a yellow monster would cause his death. Maelgwn fled to a church on the approach of the beast, but when he fearfully peeped through the keyhole the sight was enough to finish him off.

Castles of the Lesser Dynasties

Aberafan

The coastal plain between the Neath and Afan rivers in West Glamorgan has been transformed by the growth of modern industry and the most important casualty of this development was Aberafan castle, demolished in 1895 to make way for terraced housing. This castle was the centre of the surrounding lordship of Afan, a long narrow territory extending from the coast into the winding valleys of the uplands. For much of the twelfth and thirteenth centuries the descendants of Morgan ap Caradog were as hot-headed and troublesome as the other Welsh lords, but gradually they settled down and accepted English rule in return for certain rights. They prudently ingratiated themselves with their powerful neighbours, even to the extent of replacing their surnames with the curious hybrid 'de Avene'. By 1304 the rulers of Afan had established a town alongside their castle, and the territory remained under nominal Welsh control until the lordship was sold off later in the fourteenth century.

Despite the castle's long association with the Welsh, it seems far more likely that Aberafan was originally established by the Normans to control the narrow coastal route between the mountains and the sea. It was this castle that Maredudd and Rhys ap Gruffudd of Deheubarth destroyed in 1153 on behalf of their kinsman, Morgan ap Caradog. The chronicles boast how the two princes slew the garrison and carried away 'immense spoil and wealth beyond telling'. Aberafan seems to have become a replacement for Morgan's older stronghold at Plas Baglan (see below) and the castle was still intact in 1485; but just fifty years later the antiquarian John Leland failed to notice anything here, and it was certainly ruined by the end of the seventeenth century. When the site was levelled in 1895 a large chunk of masonry was removed.

Unfortunately, no detailed descriptions of the castle are known to exist and all we have to rely on is an early edition of the Ordnance Survey map to provide some clues. The 1875 map shows a large square platform with an outer ditch. Presumably this was the castle bailey, or else the buried remains of a rectangular masonry enclosure. Clearly Aberafan was a most peculiar and uncharacteristic castle, making its loss all the more regrettable.

Access: site only– the castle lay just west of St Mary's church in Port Talbot (SS 763 902).

Castell Du

Only a few tantalising fragments remain of this small thirteenth century castle, also known as Castell Rhyd-y-briw. So many walls are missing that the full plan may only ever be recovered by excavation at a future date, but given the number of modern houses crowding about the site the archaeological potential does not look very promising. The castle lies on a small hill overlooking the confluence of the rivers Senni and Usk, and appears to have had an enclosed courtyard with an apsidal tower projecting from the south side. One wall of the tower remains fairly complete, although it has been incorporated into a modern pillbox. Recent erosion of the hillside has revealed buried foundations on the western side of the tower, which might belong to the curtain wall or another tower. Could there have been a twin-towered gatehouse?

There are virtually no historical references to Castell Du other than a few letters written from here by Einion Sais, a local Welsh lord and somewhat reluctant ally of Llywelyn ap Gruffudd. By 1270 Llywelyn had extended his dominions south to Breconshire, and the castle would have been used as a base for Welsh resistance in the area. Presumably Einion was responsible for building the castle, perhaps with Llywelyn's backing. Einion is also said to have had another castle site at nearby Penpont church according to antiquarian accounts. There is, however, an intriguing reference in a contemporary chronicle to Llywelyn's 'new castle beyond Brecon', destroyed by the English in 1265. If this were one and the same, then it would suggest that the origins of Castell Du lie with the ambitious Prince of Gwynedd instead of a local lord under his thumb.

Access: on private land just south-west of Sennybridge village, on the A40 between Brecon and Llandovery. The ruins lie at the rear of some bungalows on the hill behind Sion Chapel (SN 920 284).

Castell Meredydd

Castell Meredydd was a thirteenth century stronghold of the Welsh lords of Gwynllwg, a narrow strip of land bordering the east side of Glamorgan in modern-day Monmouthshire. Like most of the ancient territorial divisions of south-east Wales, Gwynllwg comprised a fertile low-lying coastal plain, backed by bleaker uplands which remained in more or less permanent Welsh control. Several small earthwork castles in these upland areas are almost certainly native strongholds of the twelfth and early-thirteenth centuries. Few, however, make any appearance in contemporary records.

Castell Meredydd: foundations of stone buildings can be traced on the natural rocky motte

The Normans had overrun the lowlands at an early date and established a castle on the site of the Roman fort at Caerleon, and control of this strategic fort was occasionally ceded to the Welsh lords (depending on how well behaved they were!). All we know of Castell Meredydd is that it was used by Morgan ap Hywel as a retreat and back-up base when his tenuous hold on Caerleon was contested by the English. In 1236 the Brut y Tywysogion records that Gilbert Marshal, Earl of Pembroke, captured the castle during a period of truce between Llywelyn the Great and King Henry

III. By the terms of the truce Marshal was forced to return the castle to its rightful owner, which must have been particularly galling because the earl had spent a lot of money upgrading the defences. After Morgan died in 1248 the castle presumably passed to his grandson, the eponymous Maredudd, but by the end of the thirteenth century the De Clare family of Glamorgan had seized the territory and the castle was listed among the possessions of the last earl in 1314. Thereafter it disappears from the records.

The unusual topography of the site chosen by the builders resulted in yet another unique Welsh castle plan. A natural outcrop of reddish rock on an escarpment above the Rhymney valley was carved up into what can best be described as a motte and bailey. The summit of both mounds are more or less equal in height, but on the smaller eastern rock stood a round keep, while a square building or tower occupied the western peak. The stonework is now

A bird's-eye reconstruction of Castell Meredydd. Since the castle has been reduced to buried foundations, this view is highly conjectural, but it gives an impression of how it might have looked after Earl Gilbert rebuilt the outer defences

poorly preserved and mostly reduced to foundations and rubble banks, but a few upstanding pieces of the keep remains, including part of a garderobe shaft discharging over the cliff. All along the southern flank of the site the steep rocky slopes provided adequate protection, while the weaker landward approach was defended by a rectangular outer enclosure with stone walls and ditches. The gateway appears to have been on the west side of the courtyard, overlooked by a small square tower. We know that these outworks were built in 1236 because the chronicles mention that Earl Gilbert constructed 'a great fortification' around the castle. Morgan was probably responsible for the round keep and its companion building on the rocky knoll.

Access: the tree-covered remains of the castle lie on private land behind a modern house off the A468 road from Newport to Caerphilly, just north of Lower Machen village. The site can be seen by following a minor road uphill from the turning to Machen quarry (ST 226 887).

Hen Gastell

The lost castle of Morgan ap Caradog of Afan was only rediscovered as late as 1980 by archaeologists, although antiquarians had known of its existence for centuries. According to Rice Merrick (c1520-87) the castle was built by Morgan during an uprising in 1183 and lay 'upon a steep hill near to the passage of Briton Ferry', which is at the estuary of the river Neath in west Glamorgan. Until recently the site could be seen as a natural motte-like knoll, with a slight rock-cut ditch on one side isolating the flattened summit. From this windy vantage point the Welsh could control the narrow coastal route from Aberafan to Swansea and the treacherous river crossing below. Perhaps the castle had a short life, for in 1188 Gerald of Wales made the crossing in the company of Morgan, and failed to notice anything here.

Hen Gastell has been largely obliterated, and what is left of the rocky knoll now underlies the M4 motorway. Fortunately the Glamorgan-Gwent Archaeological Trust excavated the site in 1991, and discovered floor surfaces and postholes of vanished timber structures on the levelled summit. The finds included pieces of twelfth century pottery and – more surprisingly – items of Dark Age date, which suggests that Hen Gastell (like Deganwy and Dinas Emrys) was used as a defended dwelling at a much earlier period than previously suspected.

Access: Site only– the rocky outcrop can still be seen under the M4 between junctions 41 & 42, Briton Ferry, Neath (SS 731 940).

Morgraig

Of all the sites included in this book, only with Morgraig is there any doubt as to whether it is a genuine Welsh castle. It lies at the southernmost tip of the upland territory of Senghenydd, on a high ridge offering uninterrupted views across the coastal plain to Cardiff and the Bristol Channel. Ever since the site was excavated in 1903, opinions have veered towards a Welsh origin; but in recent years academics have tended to see Morgraig as an English castle. Was it an ambitious native border stronghold intimidating the Anglo-Norman territories, or an oddly designed English fortress threatening the Welsh uplands?

Tumbled walls mark out the unusual plan of Morgraig

There is hardly any historical reference to this site. During the thirteenth century the powerful De Clare family ruled Glamorgan, and the Welsh territories were conquered piecemeal by Richard de Clare (d.1262), except for Senghennydd. His son Gilbert completed the task, capturing the native ruler Gruffudd ap Rhys in 1266, and building a huge new fortress at Caerphilly two years later. Gilbert's expansionist schemes were vigorously opposed by Llywelyn ap Gruffudd who arrived at Caerphilly a few months after work began, and later burnt the unfinished structure. Although Llywelyn was defending the rights of his incarcerated vassal, he would have been more concerned about the loss of Welsh territory. Some historians believe Llywelyn was contemplating an invasion of lowland Glamorgan via Senghenydd to bring in more good agricultural land, and thereby end his dependency on the Anglesey corn supplies (it was King Edward's seizure of Anglesey that effectively starved the Welsh into submission in 1277). But his standoff against Earl Gilbert failed; Llywelyn was forced to retreat and Caerphilly castle was completed.

This is the historical context into which we must place Morgraig. It was certainly built before work started on Caerphilly, and if begun by Gruffudd then the most likely period was the four-year gap between the death of Earl Richard and his imprisonment. But could the native lord of a relatively small upland tract, have had the cash and manpower to build such an ambitious castle as Morgraig? The answer is emphatically no. However, since Llywelyn was actively involved in this area, a fortification like Morgraig would be a feasible undertaking with his backing (a similar situation was discussed above in the entry on Castell Du). Furthermore, Earl Gilbert may have arrested Gruffudd because his new castle was viewed as a serious threat to the security of English territory. But all this is conjecture; there is no hard evidence one way or another, and at present the verdict must be 'not proven'.

What the excavators dug out of the rubble in 1903 was a remarkable little fortress with an almost unique plan – a pentagonal enclosure with boldly projecting D-shaped towers on four corners, and a larger oblong keep on the fifth. It is likely that the castle was never finished and all the walls stand to a uniform height, which suggests that construction work was abruptly curtailed after just one or two building seasons. There are no signs of internal buildings or any typically Welsh rock-cut

Morgraig castle as it may have looked if completed. In this view the odd mix of Welsh and English building styles is apparent, which has left historians unsure who exactly built it

ditches. The use of strong walls with rounded towers on the angles is more characteristic of English work; but the rectangular keep, feeble gateway and absence of any ground-floor stairs (each tower had an external wooden stair to the upper chamber) – are features that would be more at home in a native stronghold. The enigma of Morgraig continues.

Access: the castle lies on the mountaintop halfway between Cardiff and Caerphilly, just off the A469, and can be reached along a footpath from the car park behind the Traveller's Rest inn (ST 160 844).

Plas Baglan

Now buried beneath centuries of debris and undergrowth, this unimpressive mound is the only major relic of the Norman-Welsh lords of Afan. The history of the De Avene clan has already been outlined in the entry for Aberafan and it is likely that Plas Baglan was their original mountain stronghold, since it lies close to the Dark Age church at Baglan. No early records specifically refer to this site (and in fact Plas Baglan was only identified as a medieval fortification by archaeologists in the 1980s), although it might have been 'the castle that once belonged to Morgan Gam' mentioned in 1245. The later history of the site is fairly well documented, for it was the seat of a minor local gentry family and was renowned as a cultural hotspot for Welsh bards and minstrels (even the great Dafydd ap Gwilym is supposed to have paid a visit). The building remained occupied into the sixteenth century, but the restricted site could not have offered much room for expansion and soon after 1600 the owners abandoned the Plas for a new house close by.

Excavation alone will recover the full plan of this intriguing site, for all that can be seen today are mounds and banks of tumbled masonry at the tip of a steep wooded ridge between two converging streams. A deep and wide ditch originally defended the vulnerable approach side, but this has almost been filled in. Here and there stony foundations can be glimpsed through the undergrowth, suggesting that the castle was a modest square enclosure with a large oblong building (either a hall or keep) at the further end. A levelled platform below the castle could be the site of a bailey. Long after Plas Baglan fell into decay, stones were robbed for use in the construction of a nearby farmhouse, which now – like the castle – is nothing more than weed-choked rubble.

Access: on private land, but visible from a nearby public footpath. From the A4211 road south of Baglan church (M4 junction 41a), follow a signposted path off Smallwood Road over the mountain to Cwm Afan (can be very muddy). After passing through a gate beside a ruined farm, the castle mound can be seen in trees at the bottom of a field on the left (SS 756 923).

Lesser castles and lost sites

Cae Castell, Neath
An odd earthwork, almost certainly belonging to the native rulers of upland Gower. It is a small rectangular enclosure backing onto a slope, with one corner of the rampart worked up into a feeble motte (SN 694 047).

Castell Bolan, Port Talbot
Another oddity, and probably built by the Welsh lords of Afan (Plas Baglan is close by). This is a type of motte with a cratered summit, perhaps marking the buried foundations of a round tower (SS 767 920).

Castell Gwern, Port Talbot

An intriguing lost site mentioned by the antiquarian Rice Merrick (c1578) as utterly ruined. Must be Welsh as it lay within the territory of Afan.

Castell Nos, Rhondda

Almost certainly a native site (and very similar to Hen Gastell) built on a typically inhospitable natural crag overlooking the upper reaches of the Rhondda Fach valley, sometime before 1247 when the Earl of Glamorgan seized the Welsh uplands. A rock-cut ditch on one side gave added defence (SN 966 001).

Dinas Powis, Barry

Excavations revealed that this twelfth-century ringwork with multiple ramparts overlies the Dark Age court of a local ruler. There is an old tradition that the last native king of Glamorgan, Iestyn ap Gwrgant, built the castle, but it was most probably a Norman foundation (ST 148 723).

Twyn Castell, Gelligaer

This little steep-sided motte stands on a ridge close to a Roman fort, and belonged to the lords of Senghenydd. From here Ifor Bach mounted a daring raid on Cardiff castle in 1158, kidnapping the Earl of Gloucester and his family, and holding them captive until all his grievances had been redressed. In 1197-8 the castle was mentioned as the seat of Cadwallon, son of Ifor (ST 137 969).

Llanhilleth

A prominent motte beside the hilltop church was probably built by the Welsh rulers of the Gwent uplands (there is an identical site not far away at Mynyddislwyn). Less obvious are a few lumps and bumps in the adjacent field where excavations in the 1920s uncovered two freestanding towers, one round, and the other of a unique cruciform plan. The site is certainly remote and odd enough to be Welsh work, but the possibility of De Clare work cannot be ruled out (SO 219 020).

References and further reading

A good general guide to Welsh history during the Age of the Princes, is Sir John Lloyd's History of Wales volume 2 (1912), while a more up to date work is R. R. Davies' Conquest, Coexistence and Change; 1063-1415 (Clarendon University Press/University of Wales Press 1987). The Governance of Gwynedd by D. Stephenson (University of Wales Press 1984) is another valuable and detailed survey of thirteenth century Welsh society. The Brut y Tywysogion is available in several translations; the one referred to here (the Peniarth version) is translated by T. Jones (University of Wales Press 1952). The published county inventories of the Royal Commission on Ancient & Historical Monuments for Wales (RCAHMW) are useful sources of further information. One of the most essential and exhaustive reference works on British castles is D. J. Cathcart King's Castellarium Anglicanum (1983). For the net surfer try J. L. Thomas' www.castlewales.com site for a colourful and detailed source of further information.

Yearly journals & academic publications:

Archaeologia Cambrensis
Archaeology in Wales
Brycheiniog
Bulletin of the Board of Celtic Studies
Carmarthenshire Antiquary
Ceredigion
Caerphilly Local History Society

Cardiff Naturalists Society
Cymmrodor
Meirioneth Historical & Record Society
Montgomeryshire Collections
Morgannwg
Pembrokeshire Historical Society

Publications:

CADW guidebooks to Welsh historic monuments – *Carreg Cennen* (J M Lewis 1990), *Criccieth* (R Avent 1989), *Denbigh* (L A Butler 1976), *Dolbadarn* (C A R Radford 1980), *Dolwyddelan* (C A R Radford 1982).

Calendar of Ancient Correspondence Concerning Wales (University of Wales Press 1935).

Castles of Mid Wales M Salter (Folly Publications 1991).

A Company of Forts P R Davis (Gomer Press 2000).

History of Cardiganshire S Meyrick (1907 edition).

History of the King's Works (HMSO 1967)

Llywelyn ap Gruffudd, Prince of Wales J B Smith (University of Wales Press 1998).

A Mirror of Medieval Wales C Knightly (CADW 1988).

Morganiae Archaeographia R Merrick (South Wales Record Society)

RCAHMW Inventories – Caernarfonshire (vol 1-3), Glamorganshire(vol 3), Meirionethshire, Montgomeryshire.

Wales and the Arthurian Legend R S Loomis (1956).

Welsh Castles; a guide by counties A Pettifer (Boydell 2000)

The Welsh Kings; the medieval rulers of Wales K Maund (Tempus 2002).

The Welsh Princes R Turvey (Longman 2002).

The Welsh Wars of Edward I J E Morris (Clarendon Press 1901).

Glossary

Aber	Welsh for an estuary or confluence of a river.
Barbican	Fortified outworks of a gatehouse.
Bastion	A projection defence work.
Caer	Welsh for a fortification (usually Iron Age or Roman).
Castell	Welsh for castle (but not always restricted to medieval sites).
Counterscarp	Additional rampart on the outer (rather than inner) edge of a defensive ditch.
Curtain wall	A high wall enclosing a castle courtyard, and linking up with towers.
Dark Age	The period between the collapse of Roman authority (c450 AD) and the Norman Conquest.
Dinas	Welsh for fortress or citadel.
Iron Age	The pre-Roman period when iron replaced the use of bronze (from c1000 BC to c100 AD).
Loop hole	A small window opening, usually wider on the inside than the outside, and designed for use by archers.
Palisade	Timber fence or stockade.
Plas	Welsh for palace (not restricted to medieval sites).
Portcullis	A metal-clad wooden grill that could be raised or lowered in front of a door.
Rampart	Raised mound or earth forming a defensive bank.
Revetment	A stone or timber facing to a rampart or slope, designed to give greater stability.
Rib vault	Raised moulding projecting from the surface of a vaulted roof.
Tomen	Welsh for a mound (usually a medieval motte).
Ward	Another name for the courtyard or bailey of a stone castle.